The Poetry and Prose of E. E. Cummings

Robert E. Wegner

The

Poetry

and

Prose

of

E. E. CUMMINGS

Harcourt, Brace & World, Inc.

New York

The author wishes to thank the following for permission to quote
from the works of E. E. Cummings:

Marion Morehouse Cummings and Harcourt, Brace & World, Inc.,
for passages from *Poems 1923–1954, 95 Poems,* and *73 Poems* by E. E.
Cummings; from *Adventures in Value by* Marion Morehouse and E. E.
Cummings; from *E. E. Cummings: A Miscellany,* edited by George J.
Firmage. Copyright © 1923, 1925, 1931, 1935, 1938, 1940, 1944, 1946,
1950, 1951, 1953, 1954, 1955, 1957, 1958, 1959, 1960, 1961 by E. E.
Cummings; © 1962 by Marion Morehouse; Copyright © 1963 by
Marion Morehouse Cummings.

Harvard University Press, for passages from *i:six nonlectures.* Copyright 1953 by E. E. Cummings.

For my mother

Acknowledgments

Like most projects this study is not the product of one intelligence or single source of energy. I owe gratitude to my wife, Phyllis, for her typing and retyping, to Dr. Lyon N. Richardson for his guidance and encouragement in the initial stages of writing, to Norman Friedman and David V. Forrest for their helpful suggestions both specific and general, and to Mrs. Joan Kimball Yehl for her perseverance in proofreading and copy editing. I am indebted to the many authors of articles on Cummings' works in a way which I cannot exactly assess. Without doubt the manner in which I have treated the poems and prose has been influenced, to some extent at least, by earlier studies. I have drawn upon some of the ideas and statements of these writers; for their observations and insights I offer my appreciation.

E. E. Cummings corresponded with me about this book. We talked about it in his apartment. He read the manuscript and told me that he "enjoyed it greatly." His interest and enthusiasm for the work as well as letters of encouragement from Marion Morehouse, his wife, lightened the task of writing and revising. My gratitude is to the memory of the man—and the poet.

Poems and portions of poems are identified in the text of this study by first line and the title of the original volume in which the poem appeared. At present, all of Cummings' poems published before 1954 are included in *Poems: 1923– 1954,* where they are grouped according to the separate volumes. His later poems appear in *95 Poems* (1958) and *73 Poems* (1963). A chronological list of Cummings' books published in America is included as an appendix.

Contents

The material was pure, and his art was pure;
how could the result be other than wonderful?
—Thoreau, *Walden,* XVIII

The Poetry and Prose of E. E. Cummings

Introduction

Works of art are of an infinite loneliness and with nothing to be so little reached as with criticism. Only love can grasp and hold and fairly judge them.

—RAINER MARIA RILKE

Cummings quoted the above passage in his first "nonlecture," at Harvard University in 1952, adding, "In my proud and humble opinion, those two sentences are worth all the soi-disant criticism of the arts which has ever existed or will ever exist." In a conversation on December 20, 1955, he told me that he thought critics got worked up over his poetry because they could not fit it into a category. "Critics, evidently, find it difficult to classify my poems in some way. This seems to be the difficulty that people have reading my poetry." He went on to say that a poem has its own life and that regardless of what anyone might say about a particular poem of his, the poem would continue to exist.

Cummings' poetry has been the subject of much critical investigation. In 1962 Norman Friedman compiled a list of essays and reviews pertaining to Cummings' works that filled fourteen single-spaced typewritten pages—a sizable bibliography for a poet to acquire in his lifetime.

From the beginning his unusual techniques and stylistic devices attracted attention, and in succeeding years critics have concerned themselves mainly with his typographical eccentricities: his peculiar line arrangements, his freedom with commas and other marks of punctuation, his displacement of words, and his disregard of standard practice in the use of capital letters. Needless to say, opinion differs over the merits of his technical innovations.

Critics have paid far less attention to Cummings' subject matter, themes, and ideas. Here again, opinion is divided. Some critics have dismissed his subject matter as easily perceived or juvenile, his themes as conventional or oversimplified, his ideas as of little depth or significance. Others find the whole of his poetry profoundly impressive. They see Cummings as an outstanding lyric poet and find in his glorification of the individual a needed corrective to the widespread tendency to equate majority opinion with right and mass production with progress.

During the mid-fifties, when interest in Cummings' technical practice was at its height, Rudolph Von Abele, Louis Calvin Rus, and Robert Lawrence Beloof published studies dealing with grammatical displacement, structural ambiguities, and the various prosodic forms and shapes Cummings employed. Except for Beloof's study, however, these examinations exist in something of a vacuum; that is to say, they are exhaustive compilations of the devices he employed, but the information reveals nothing about Cummings' themes, his subject matter, or his own temperament or attitude.

In 1960 Norman Friedman published the first full-scale discussion of Cummings' poetry under the title, *E. E. Cummings: The Art of his Poetry*. It is a valuable book, for it moves far toward integrating subject matter and themes with Cummings' poetic technique. Moreover, this study illustrates and explains many of the poet's unique devices, such as his coinage of words.

In 1964 two more books on Cummings were published, another by Norman Friedman called *e. e. cummings: The Growth of a Writer* and a study by Barry Marks simply titled *E. E. Cummings*. Friedman describes his second book as an "introductory survey," and in a sensitive introduction he defines Cummings' thematic views. The rest of the book is given over to an examination of Cummings' major prose and poetry publications with the purpose of demonstrating the poet's development as a writer. Mr. Marks' study is particularly welcome and interesting for what it reveals about Cummings' aesthetic views. Cummings was also a graphic artist and his absorption in some of the most advanced principles of art affected his poetic style, as Mr. Marks convincingly demonstrates.

From a reading of Cummings' critics it is clear, at least, that his poetry and prose affect persons strongly, that no one reacts with indifference. Since his early volumes attracted widespread attention with their ebullience and flair, his work often served as a focus for controversy over the aims and methods of the modernists. Ezra Pound alludes to the crux of this controversy in *Canto 89:*

"You damn sadist!" said mr. cummings,
           "you try to make people think."

Pound is amused, I think, but R. P. Blackmur and F. O. Matthiessen, critics in the T. S. Eliot camp of poetry, interpreted Cummings' anti-intellectual attitude as anything except amusing. Many younger critics, however, defended Cummings' practice and stance. Karl Shapiro, for example, in an exceptionally fine article, "Prosody as the Meaning" (*Poetry,* March, 1949), refers to Cummings' famous and much anthologized poem on Buffalo Bill to demonstrate that poetry is not a vehicle for conveying knowledge or information, that a poem is without *meaning* in any functional sense of the word. Mr. Shapiro asserts that *in the poem* the number of clay pigeons broken by Buffalo Bill, "onetwothreefourfive" (not the same thing as five), cannot be thought of as meaningful except as art.

Cummings told me that when he saw the act Buffalo Bill used a rifle. An eye-witness of another performance writes that "as Buffalo Bill careened with breakneck speed around the ring, attendants would toss glass balls into the air, and, lightning-like, he would whip out his six-shooter from his holster, and instantaneously you would hear the boom of his gun—and shattered bits of glass would float to the sawdust. Six shots, six shattered balls! He never missed." [1]

The accounts vary. The point here is that poetry is meaningful as performance, not as fact. To Buffalo Bill's youthful admirers, none of whom could probably hit the broadside of a barn with a rifle or a revolver while astride a galloping horse, the number of clay pigeons shot down was probably not important at all. To them the exciting aspect

[1] M. M. Marberry, "Buffalo Bill Was a Great Man," in *New World Writing: 8th Mentor Selection* (New York: New American Library, 1955), p. 139.

6

was that he did shoot them down, regardless of the number. This is the point, I think, that Mr. Shapiro is making about poetry in general and some of Cummings' poems in particular—that it is the performance and not the fact that is exciting.

The interest that Cummings has excited among readers and critics may be noted by the number of poets and writers to whom he has been compared. This proclivity for noting echoes and similarities between poets and poems, apparently inspired by Matthew Arnold's touchstone method of criticism, was rife during the early decades of our century. Cummings came in for his share. He has been compared to Emerson, Blake, Ezra Pound, Apollinaire, Mina Loy, Marianne Moore, William Carlos Williams, Swinburne, Chaucer, Spenser, Shakespeare, Gerard Manley Hopkins, Shelley, Herbert, John Dryden, James Joyce, Daniel Defoe, John Donne, Wordsworth, and T. S. Eliot. He has been related to such schools or modes of poetry as the seventeenth-century metaphysical poets, the Elizabethan sonneteers and the Elizabethan song tradition, the Imagists, the Romantics, and the Pre-Raphaelites. It is hard to say what all this proves: certainly no one is contending that Cummings is a derivative poet. The only conclusion one can come to is that he has read widely in English poetry and prose and has appreciated it.

Cummings himself indicated some of his direct sources of influence: he tells us, for example, in *i:six nonlectures,* that he wrote sonnets from the time he became acquainted with those of Rossetti. He tells us that Nashe's song, "Spring the sweet spring, is the year's pleasant king" from the masque *Summer's Last Will and Testament,* is a poem he loved "even more than if [it] were my own. . . ." The reader may feel that there is some similarity, perhaps even a striking similarity, between this poem by Nashe and one by Cummings in *1 × 1* that begins: "sweet spring is your/ time is my time is our/ time." In conversation he told me that one of his favorite poems was Herrick's "Violets." "I love the poem," he said. In my own reading of Cummings, I noticed a similarity between one of the poems in *1 × 1* and a ballad usually considered to be Thomas Campion's. The similarity exists only in the first lines. Campion's runs:

What if a day, or a month, or a year

Cummings' line reads:

what if a much of a which of a wind

The two lines are identical in prosody and in the use of the first three words. Beyond this the two poems are not at all alike.

A phrase which I assume Cummings coined and found intriguing is "the square root of minus one." He used it in at least three different contexts. In his book *EIMI,* published in 1933, he wrote: "Russian equals English equals square root of minus 1." In 1936, in what he published as a "Speech (From a Forthcoming Play)," we find this sentence: "Not something dreamed—no one, anyone, can guess that; even a physicing mathematician with his hand on the square root of minus one and his mind at the back of his own neck." Finally, in the well-known Introduction to his *Collected Poems* of 1938 he wrote: "Mostpeople have less in common with ourselves than the squarerootofminusone." This phrase, because it is unusual, stuck in my mind and recalled a similar phrase which De Quincey used in much the same way: "Space, again—what is it in most men's minds? The lifeless form of the world without us, a postulate of the geometrician, with no more vitality or real existence to their feelings than the square root of two."[2] I was rather elated to discover this similarity, but what it proves amounts to exactly the square root of minus one: less than nothing.

I had another adventure in literary detection while reading Gerard Manley Hopkins' poem, "The May Magnificat." I was particularly struck by the following lines:

> Question: What is Spring?
> Growth in every thing—
>
> Flesh and fleece, fur and feather,
> Grass and greenworld all together;
> Star-eyed strawberry-breasted
> Throstle above her nested
>
> .   .   .   .   .
>
> Well but there was more than this:
> Spring's universal bliss
> Much, had much to say
> To offering Mary May.

It might be proposed, after comparing this and the following poem, that Cummings took the image "strawberry-breasted" from Hopkins and applied it to a girl in her puberty; that he took the definition of spring, "Growth in

[2] "Concerning Literature," in *The Art of Literary Criticism,* ed. by Paul Robert Lieder and Robert Withington (New York: Appleton-Century-Crofts, 1951), p. 442.

9

every thing," and applied it to the physical development of a young woman instead of to Nature's praise of the Virgin Mary; and finally that he took the word-play on "Much" (that is, abundance) having "much" and transformed it into an equation of "much and much," a really sensuous line suggesting natural growth. Thus, Cummings' poem (from *XAIPE*):

> if the
>
> green
> opens
> a little a
> little
> was
> much and much
> is
>
> too if
>
> the green robe
> o
> p
> e
> n
> s
> and two are
>
> wildstrawberries

Whether Cummings employed any of the phraseology or imagery of Hopkins is irrelevant; what is relevant is that Cummings wrote a poem that is entirely his own, stamped with his personal touch and flair, even though isolated echoes may be traced back to a predecessor. Fascinating as it may be to note similarities (or the lack of them) in image, phrase, subject matter, theme, or poetic device among poets, this practice contributes little toward a genuine understanding of Cummings' poetry.

My purpose in this book is to present an *appreciation* of Cummings as a poet. I have not made lists, graphs, or charts. I have simply commented upon those elements in the prose and poetry of Cummings that have interested me, particularly the interrelationship of his themes, subject matter, images, and techniques. This study differs from earlier ones in that I have assumed that the poems can be understood only in and for themselves, one at a time. Like John Ciardi, I am convinced that "to read any one poem carefully is the ideal preparation for reading another."

In the opening chapters of this study, which are important as prelude to a discussion of Cummings' themes, I have attempted to demonstrate that in Cummings' work there is a particularly close association between experience and art. Although a number of critics think differently, Cummings does have a system of thought which often strikes the reader as difficult because of its very simplicity.

This study is not an inclusive treatment of all that exists in Cummings' works. But it is an attempt to bring more than one aspect or element into a related perspective. I hope, naturally, that the interested reader finds through these pages that his own appreciation of the poet will increase.

1. Identity of the Artist

After this moment, the question "who am I?" is answered by what I write—in other words, I become my writing; and my autobiography becomes the exploration of my stance as a writer.

—i:six nonlectures

Cummings is here saying that the artist discovers himself through his art. The poet writes out of his own experience: the discipline of poetry, acting upon that experience, increases awareness, perception, understanding. It is in this manner that the poet becomes his writing. He becomes that greater awareness of the meaning or mystery of his existence which the demands of his art awake in him. To use a simple illustration, Cummings discovers, in writing a birthday poem to his beloved, that her birthday is his blessing, hence his own birthday (see Poem 62 in *95 Poems*). Paradox such as this is the staple of his work: his poems are new views of known things.

For Cummings, self-discovery was supremely important and the only valid motive for writing a poem; it separated his awareness from stereotyped awarenesses, separated his identity as an artist from his conventional identity as a member of society. If the truth of human existence is to be uncovered and recognized, it will be accomplished through the perspective of the artist. As Cummings said in his comment in Oscar Williams' anthology, *The War Poets:* ". . . only the artist in yourselves is more truthful than the night."

The process of self-discovery is like swimming upstream against the current; it demands continuous effort and constant attention. Like the swimmer, the artist deals with the transient and the fluid in time and space; in this flux he attempts to find meaning and personal truths. He does this by expressing himself artistically, by writing a poem, by imposing form upon the apparent chaos of existence. In the process of writing a poem, the poet discovers his identity, which paradoxically is one of fusion and harmony with the eternal forces of change. The artist discovers his identity in the eternal by resisting the current of temporal affairs; at the same time, it is in the temporal world that the artist discovers the eternal and spiritual. This unfolding of identity is never-ending: it depends upon an honest appraisal of felt experience.

Given his high view of the artist's function, it is not difficult to understand why Cummings had scorn for those who write out of anything other than genuine experience. In the following poem (from *W* [*ViVa*]) it is probably not just coincidental that S. S. Van Dine (a writer whose impossible heroes of detective fiction were popular in the 1920's) is indirectly associated with that eighteenth-century faker, James Macpherson, through the phonetic allusion to Ossian ("o.c.an") and through the three-way pun on the word

"dine." The use of the coprologous French expletive "merde"
is the coup de grâce to Philo Vance.

> murderfully in midmost o.c.an
>
> launch we a Hyperluxurious Supersieve
> (which Ultima Thule Of Plumbing shall receive
>
> the philophilic name S.S. VAN MERDE)
>
> having first put right sleuthfully aboard
> all to—mendaciously speaking—a man
>
> wrongers who write what they are dine to live

Cummings was the son of parents who were devoted to
each other and to him. His father was the Reverend Edward
Cummings, Harvard University professor and noted Uni-
tarian minister. His mother came from an austere and
highly respectable family, "Roxbury stock" according to
Cummings in *i:six nonlectures*. However, Cummings'
mother more than anyone else represented joy to him; he
describes her as the most "completely and humanly and un-
affectedly generous" person he had ever known. Cummings
writes that she "breathed" and "smiled" her Unitarianism.

The happiness of Cummings' early life, his sense of being
loved, and his devotion to his parents have found expression in many poems. Two of the most obvious and best
known are the famous elegies: "my father moved through
dooms of love" (*50 Poems*) and "if there are any heavens
my mother will(all by herself)have" (*W* [*ViVa*]). The
ideal or near ideal love that he felt existed between his
parents is celebrated in the poem "anyone lived in a pretty
how town" (*50 Poems*). His admiration for his father is

nowhere so freely stated as in a letter Cummings wrote to Paul Rosenfeld, reproduced in *i:six nonlectures*. Some of the ideals he attributed to his father appear in such poems as "a man who had fallen among thieves" (*is 5*), "conceive a man,should he have anything" (*no thanks*), and "who sharpens every dull" (*XAIPE*); and in "nonlecture three," he said: "As it was my miraculous fortune to have a true father and a true mother, and a home which the truth of their love made joyous, so—in reaching outward from this love and this joy—I was marvellously lucky to touch and seize a rising and striving world; . . ."

Cummings went to Harvard College, where he took his B.A. in 1915 and his M.A. in 1916. He majored in Greek and the classics. He told me that he had been reading Greek ever since for the fun of it—although he still could not read it at sight. In *Adventures in Value* (III, 4) he mentions that he memorized the Greek alphabet as a small boy, not without some struggle. In the same book he speaks of the Greek classics as "that noblest realm,of Pindar & of Aeschylus, whose values are & were & will remain man's true spiritual home" (IV, 9). Two of his book titles, *EIMI* (I am) and *XAIPE* (Rejoice), further reflect his familiarity with Greek.

The concept of love as a positive force to be equated with joy and growth had its source in Cummings' experience as a child; he grew up in an aura of love. From the same source, from his study of Greek literature, and no doubt from other sources, came his conviction of the essential dignity of the individual. Both are central to his writing. Love is the propelling force behind a great body of his poetry. In time he came to see love and the dignity of the human being as inseparable. Love, according to Cummings, abolishes class barriers, among them the barrier that is assumed to exist between servants and those who employ them. In *i:six nonlectures* he says that in his boyhood home the servants "were not slaves. . . . they were loved and loving human beings." He concludes with a general statement that explains his many satiric thrusts at headwaiters and others in service jobs in America and Russia: ". . . slavery, and the only slavery, is service without love." In many poems and in the travel diary *EIMI,* Cummings touches upon the pathetic existence of those people (servants, waiters, street cleaners, etc.) who are "notalive" because they are neither loved nor capable of loving. For example, consider this description of a headwaiter in Odessa in the Hotel London: "With a dignity quite at right angles to both that dumb lusting after selfhumiliation and that assertive dread of selfabasement which respectively afflict unmen in general and headwaiters in particular."

Cummings' notions about the worth of love and the dignity of the human being are not unrelated to the distinction he makes between a house and a home. In *i:six nonlectures* Cummings explains this distinction. In the play *Him* and the morality play *Santa Claus* he dramatizes it. Cummings conceived of a home as a refuge from the pseudo realities of the exterior world, a place of privacy where the individual may be himself. In contrast, the modern house is often anything but a sanctum; instead, with its picture windows and its innumerable gadgets and devices, it seems designed to admit as much of the exterior world as possible.

In the play *Him* Cummings symbolizes this contrast between a home and a house by means of a nonexistent wall.

Since the original intention of a wall is outmoded, he uses the nonexistent wall both as stage prop and as symbol. He explains the significance of walls in *i:six nonlectures:* "Even supposing that (from time to time) walls exist around you, those walls are no longer walls; they are merest pseudosolidities, perpetually penetrated by the perfectly predatory collective organs of sight and sound." Symbolically the play presents the dilemma of the sensitive individual in the modern world, identifying himself with the exterior world yet maintaining fidelity to his inner being. This same problem is the crux of *Santa Claus,* but with one significant distinction: the application has been changed from the individual to the mass public. In brief, *Santa Claus* suggests that faith in external values, which are neither real nor valid, can lead only to a dead end.

Cummings' satiric thrusts at his conventional New England background with its decorum, propriety, and respectability spring from the same source as his poems of eulogy and joy—namely his convictions about love and human dignity. Cummings defends these values against any force or idea that would threaten them. Rules and regulations about what is correct and proper stifle spontaneity, thwart joy, stunt spiritual growth; they may prevent love, may prevent the realization of one's dignity. You cannot know who you are if you are concerned only with what society demands that you should be. Hence Cummings ridicules the stuffy elements of his own New England, Puritan heritage. In "nonlecture two" he says: "I had every socalled reason to accept these conventional distinctions without cavil; yet for some unreason I didn't." He goes on to explain that his education as a poet depended upon his exploration of the world beyond the limits of Cambridge. The neighboring town of Somerville had a reputation entirely different from that of Cambridge. Cummings continues:

. . . The more implacably a virtuous Cambridge drew me toward what might have been her bosom, the more sure I felt that soi-disant respectability comprised nearly everything which I couldn't respect, and the more eagerly I explored sinful Somerville. But while sinful Somerville certainly possessed a bosom (in fact, bosoms) she also possessed fists which hit below the belt and arms which threw snowballs containing small rocks. Little by little and bruise by teacup, my doubly disillusioned spirit made an awe-inspiring discovery; which (on more than several occasions) has prevented me from wholly misunderstanding socalled humanity: the discovery, namely, that all groups, gangs, and collectivities—no matter how apparently disparate—are fundamentally alike; and that what makes any world go round is not the trivial difference between a Somerville and a Cambridge, but the immeasurable difference between either of them and individuality.

One of Cummings' poetic jokes at the expense of his proper Cambridge heritage is embodied in a poem from *is 5* that by implication contrasts the decorous respectability of Cambridge with the atmosphere of a night club—in Somerville, in Boston, it hardly matters where. The poem contrasts two persons: "dolores," a fan dancer, and Professor Royce of Harvard University. In "nonlecture two" Cummings tells an anecdote about the absent-minded Professor Royce. He had the habit of starting off to his classes at the college without his tie. "Josie! Josie!" his wife would yell, and run after him, "waving something stringlike in her dexter fist. Mr Royce politely paused, allowing his spouse to catch up with him; he then shut both eyes, while she snapped around his collar a narrow necktie possessing a permanent bow; his eyes thereupon opened, he bowed, she smiled, he advanced, she retired, and the scene was over."

In the poem, "dolores" represents the pagan atmosphere of the night club. The chorus girl consciously puts herself in a state of dishabille, the professor does so unconsciously. Both of the worlds represented by the two figures are valid and perhaps dependent upon each other, as suggested by the pun on the word "Royce" which lends unity to the poem and strengthens the claim of each world for recognition.

> curtains part)
> the peacockappareled
> prodigy of Flo's midnight
> Frolic dolores
>
> small in the head keen chassised like a Rolls
> Royce
> swoops smoothly
>   outward(amid
> tinkling-cheering-hammering
>
> tables)
>
> while softly along Kirkland Street
> the infantile ghost of Professor
> Royce rolls
>
> remembering that it
>
> has for
> -gotten some-
> thing ah
>
> (my
>
> necktie

A large number of the allusions in his poems to Puritan sobriety and dignity take the form of satiric comments or irreverent remarks, as in the two following excerpts from poems in *is 5:*

> my uncle Ed
> that's
> dead from the neck
>
> up is lead all over
> Brattle Street by a castrated pup

and:

> . . . a watermelon causes indigestion to William Cullen Long-fellow's small negro son, Henry Wadsworth Bryant.

or this, from *50 Poems:*

> harder perhaps than a newengland bed

or this, from *Tulips and Chimneys:*

> the Cambridge ladies who live in furnished souls
> are unbeautiful and have comfortable minds
>
> .   .   .   .   .
>
> they believe in Christ and Longfellow, both dead,

Cummings' typographical oddities also may express his rebellion against his New England heritage of proper conduct and academic rigidity.

Soon after graduating from Harvard, Cummings joined the Norton-Harjes Ambulance Corps, serving in France during the First World War. One fruit of his war experiences and subsequent confinement in a French prison was *The Enormous Room,* probably his most widely read book. He also wrote a number of war poems which are powerful, ironic comments on the inhumanity, horror, and cruelty of mechanized warfare.

Both before and after his service in the ambulance corps Cummings studied painting in New York and Paris. He received recognition as a painter as early as 1931 when a limited edition of 391 copies of his works in charcoal, ink, oil, pencil, and watercolor was published under the title *CIOPW.* This training had its most noticeable effect on the typographical and visual appearance of his poems. Many of them present astonishing forms. Some are designed to be read vertically on the page instead of horizontally; in others stanzaic structures are balanced as masses are balanced in paintings; one poem looks like a football standing on end; the dedication of the volume *no thanks* is in the pattern of a wine glass; perhaps the most pictorial of them (from *XLI Poems*) resembles smoke puffing and billowing out of a locomotive:

```
        the
          sky
              was
        can   dy lu
        minous
              edible
        spry
             pinks shy
        lemons
        greens   coo   l choc
        olate
        s.
```

un   der,
a   lo
co
mo
tive   s pout
ing
vi
o
lets

Other evidences of Cummings' familiarity with the visual arts may be found in his reference to El Greco (in the Foreword to *is 5*) and to the early Picasso to whom he wrote an entire poem; in his use of such terms as "metope" and "triglyph"; and in the use of aesthetics as satiric subject matter, particularly in relation to statues. In another of his poems he has phonetically inscribed his own signature: "hErE cOmEs a glass box . . ." This calls to mind the Renaissance painter, who sometimes signed his works by inserting his own portrait as a minor figure in a group.

The impact of New York City on Cummings was, by his own admission, inestimable. New York came to him as a "phenomenon and a miracle. . . . in New York I also breathed: and as if for the first time."

. . . The phenomenon was a telemicroscopic chimera, born of the satanic rape of matter by mind; a phallic female phantasm, clothed in thunderous anonymity and adorned with colossally floating spiderwebs of traffic; a stark irresistibly stupendous newness, mercifully harboring among its pitilessly premeditated spontaneities immemorial races and nations [*i:six nonlectures*]

In New York Cummings found inspiration and subject matter for many poems, for at least one of his prose sketches

("Mr. X"), and for the play *Him*. In New York there are people who are "alive," who recognize the truth of living, and who respond with joy to the world around them. Then there is the city itself, its thunderstorms and its sunsets. Out of his experience came poems on burlesque shows, strip-tease dancers such as Sally Rand, entertainers such as Jimmy Savo, circus performers, organ grinders with monkeys on strings, blind beggars, the vitality of colored people, Chinese laundrymen, and the wonderful effects of twilight and sunrise on steel and concrete structures. Just as numerous, however, are poems that reveal the deadening influences of the city. There are poems (some of them satiric, some vividly realistic) about depraved people: whores, derelicts, "hardboil guys," the "muckers pimps and tratesmen," the "famous fatheads." He castigates salesmen, businessmen, politicians, advertisers and advertising slogans; he ridicules public reactions to celebrities, official parades, and religious processions. For the mechanized response to life Cummings has only scorn.

In comparison with his response to New York, Cummings' reaction to Paris was almost wholly positive. He states in *i:six nonlectures* that in Paris he "participated in an actual marriage of material with immaterial things; I celebrated an immediate reconciling of spirit and flesh, forever and now, heaven and earth. Paris was for me precisely and complexly this homogeneous duality: this accepting transcendence; this living and dying more than death or life. Whereas—by the very act of becoming its improbably gigantic self—New York had reduced mankind to a tribe of pygmies, Paris (in each shape and gesture and avenue and cranny of her being) was continuously expressing the humanness of humanity." A briefer eulogy of Paris occurs in *The Enormous Room* at that point in the narrative where Cummings, under guard, passes through the city en route to prison. "A great shout came up from every insane drowsy brain that had travelled with us—a fierce and beautiful cry, which went the length of the train. . . . Paris where one forgets, Paris which is Pleasure, Paris in whom our souls live, Paris the beautiful, . . ." Yet for all of the humane splendor and inspiration that Cummings attributes to Paris, it does not compare to New York as a source of motivation and material for his art.

In 1931 Cummings took a trip through the U.S.S.R. which resulted in a travel diary called *EIMI,* published in 1933. In the Introduction to the Modern Library edition of *The Enormous Room* (1932), Cummings wrote: "Eimi is the individual again; a more complex individual, a more enormous room." *EIMI,* like *The Enormous Room,* glorifies individual freedom. The book, published at a time when it was considered progressive to praise Communism, is an exposé of the loss of human vitality that occurs when people are subjugated to collectivism and mechanical regimentation. Twenty years later, commenting again on conditions as he observed them in Russia and on the concept of Communism, this time in *i:six nonlectures,* he expressed the same opinion: "So much (or so little) for one major aspect of the inhuman unworld: a fanatical religion of irreligion, conceived by sterile intellect and nurtured by omnipotent nonimagination. . . . this gruesome apotheosis of mediocrity in the name of perfectibility, this implacable salvation of all through the assassination of each, this reasoned enormity of spiritual suicide. . . ." The noticeable difference between *The Enormous Room* and *EIMI* lies in the scope of their implications: whereas *The Enormous Room* revealed cruelty and suffering inflicted upon innocent human beings by war, *EIMI* reveals the inhumanity of an ideology imposed upon a people under the banner of materialistic progress.

He writes in *EIMI:*

"I said:in the days of the Tzar,a Russian's soul was his passport;now"(medium shot of rattler, its back broken by small rock, spiralling)"his soul belongs to the government."

And again:

". . . I begin seriously to wonder if noone in Russia must actually be near anyone,if everyone must from everyone else keep that meaningly infinite distance known as Altruism. . . ."

A trenchant and funny poem published in *no thanks* (1935) sums up his response to Communist Russia. The last stanza reads:

> every kumrad is a bit
> of quite unmitigated hate
> (travelling in a futile groove
> god knows why)
> and so do i
> (because they are afraid to love

Throughout his career Cummings insisted that the artist must maintain fidelity to himself. In *i:six nonlectures* he says: ". . . if poetry is your goal, you've got to forget all about punishments and all about rewards and all about self-styled obligations and duties and responsibilities etcetera

25

ad infinitum and remember one thing only: that it's you—nobody else—who determine your destiny and decide your fate. Nobody else can be alive for you; nor can you be alive for anybody else. . . . There's the artist's responsibility; and the most awful responsibility on earth."

The most extended analysis of the problem of maintaining individuality as a man and fidelity to self as an artist occurs in the play *Him*. The term *man* may be equated with the modes and requirements of the exterior social world, the term *artist* with the interior or intuitive truths of the human heart. The dramatic tension of the play rises from the struggle of the character Him to determine what is genuine and what is false, what truly exists and what he is deceived into thinking exists. According to Him, his existence is based on three cardinal tenets, and the ability to live simultaneously by them he likens to the agility required of a circus performer to sit astride three chairs, stacked one on top of the other, balanced on a high wire. The necessity of balancing on these three chairs in order to achieve a progressive recognition of self and complete individuality, and the significance of these chairs, are explained by Him to his lover, Me. "The three chairs are three facts—it [Him's conviction] will quickly kick them out from under itself and will stand on air; and in that moment (because everyone will be disappointed) everyone will applaud. Meanwhile, some thousands of miles over everyone's head, over a billion empty faces, it rocks carefully and smilingly on three things, on three facts, on: I am an Artist, I am a Man, I am a Failure—it rocks and it swings and it smiles and it does not collapse tumble or die because it pays no attention to anything except itself."

This image suggests a kind of perfection (without props or support) in harmony and balance. Metaphorically, a spiritual fusion with universal will has been achieved. But why failure? In Him's triad, the topmost chair is failure.

To understand the significance of *failure,* it is helpful to refer to another word that occurs throughout the poet's works. That word is *nothing.* Although these terms are not synonymous as Cummings uses them, they do have some meaning in common. Both words are paradoxical. *Failure,* as Him uses the word, is inevitable. Since the Artist-Man all but succeeds in his creative endeavor, the word describing his accomplishment is *failure.* But *failure* here has no pejorative sense. Rather, for Him, who has kicked the three balanced chairs out from beneath the conviction of what he is, *failure* is the miracle of walking on air. It describes the status of the Artist-Man who has attained spiritual harmony with the universal will or impulse which informs all creation. In this respect, *failure* represents a kind of success.

The concept of *nothing* is important in Cummings' works, for it is the value of *nothing* that the Artist-Man continually tries to capture in his poems. Like *failure,* the word *nothing* as Cummings uses it does not have a pejorative sense. Paradoxically, *nothing* is the term Cummings often applies to everything that represents the truest in values and significance. *Nothing* is that which is not tangible; for Cummings the word may be equated with the invisible harmony, mystery, and perfection of the universe. Through his poetry the Artist-Man attempts to capture the essence of *nothing*— and fails. He fails because no poem is finally capable of replacing the physical or inherent spiritual quality of the object or situation described. The poem only attempts to do so—and in this attempt *failure* is inherent. But through *failure* the Artist-Man approaches *nothing*—he becomes one with the spiritual truth of his existence. He accomplishes the miracle of walking on air, realizes the transcendental experience of becoming eternally involved with the universal spirit of love and creation. Cummings says, in his Introduction to *The Enormous Room,* that people who are not artists "don't become: . . . I feel negation becomes of them."

Evidences of this concept of the artist may be found in Cummings' poetry. The first two steps in Him's progressive triad (Artist and Man) relate the problem of balancing the interior recognition of beauty and harmony felt by the artist with the exterior events and man-made forces perceived by the man. The artist unavoidably works with ideas, but for the genuine expression of these ideas he depends upon the man and his ability to interpret the messages of the five senses properly. Hence we have a fusion: the artist is the man; the man is the artist. Neither, by himself, could achieve individuality and recognition of self, for the artist without the man would be sterile and lifeless, and the man without the artist would misinterpret what he perceives through the senses. Without the qualifying temperament of the artist, the man would have little resistance to stereotyped beliefs. With the artist and his inner recognition of truth, beauty, and harmony, the man through his senses perceives the manifestations of these in the world around him, and learns to distinguish between what is genuine and what is sham and hypocrisy. As has been noted, much of Cummings' poetry satirizes the falseness and hypocrisy he found in the world; but the perceptions of the man tempered by the insight of the artist also found those realities in the world that are celebrated in his poetry as love (human and spiritual), compassion, spontaneity, joy, freedom, and the truths of the senses.

Failure, the third step in Him's triad toward a recognition of self and ultimate inclusion in the universal harmony of *nothing,* can be more clearly understood by reference to some of the poems and a statement Cummings made in the Foreword to *is 5.* Cummings' *failure* is akin to Browning's thesis that it is not the attainment but the striving for it that has value. Fra Lippo Lippi alludes to it when he notes that the function of art is to revitalize the objects of nature, which human beings have forgotten how to look at, let alone love and appreciate. Cummings would ascribe this human failing to the substitution of a belief about an object for its actuality. However, in the very process of restoring true dimension and meaning, the Artist-Man is doomed to *failure,* according to Cummings—for the artistic reproduction of an object is not the object itself. At best it is a reflection of the original—as in these lines from a poem in *is 5:*

> if i have made,my lady,intricate
> imperfect various things chiefly which wrong
> your eyes(frailer than most deep dreams are frail)
> songs less firm than your body's whitest song
> upon my mind—if i have failed to snare
> the glance too shy—if through my singing slips
> the very skillful strangeness of your smile
> the keen primeval silence of your hair
>
> —let the world say "his most wise music stole
> nothing from death"—

In the Foreword to *is 5* Cummings says that the poet is one "who is obsessed by Making," and that "It is with roses and locomotives (not to mention acrobats Spring electricity Coney Island the 4th of July the eyes of mice and Niagara Falls) that my 'poems' are competing." The word *competing* is important, for it suggests the interpretation Cummings places on the word *failure:* the finest poem about a rose will never equal the rose itself. However, it is the artist's privilege, duty, and joy to perceive the object's peculiar and identifying essence, which hitherto has been unrecognized by men or has been lost through misconception. Cummings found that the concepts or rationalizations applied to the original phenomenon or object often had disfigured or disguised its true form or essence beyond recognition. The poet, by reidentifying that which he writes about, reveals truth, maintains his individuality, and discovers himself. And it is through this process of combining the Man's perceptions of external reality with the Artist's recognitions of truth and beauty, in the realization that the human endeavor of re-creation must end in *failure,* that the poet achieves the pinnacle of *nothingness*—spiritual accord with the informing impulse of the universe.

To this point we have been dealing with Cummings' mystique. Two key words in Cummings' mystique are *failure* and *nothing*. These two words help clarify each other. *Nothing* represents the spirit or essence of existence; it is no thing. For Cummings the apparent confusion and chaos of the visible and tangible world dissolves when one becomes aware of the spiritual world inherent in it. The task of the poet is to attempt to come to grips with this world of spirit, to show that behind the tumultuous and disparate impressions lies a world of harmony, order, and unity of spirit. This world is more real than the superficial world of unrelated sense impressions: it is the world of *nothing,* wherein lies the truth of our existence. As an example, let us suppose that the flight of a bird stirs both the Artist and the Man to try to capture its significance. For the Man there is the visual impression of symmetry, co-ordination, hovering balance—all physical attributes of the bird in action. For the Artist, however, these same attributes suggest the beauty, harmony, perfection of which they are a part, and bring a brief realization of the essence of the bird's flight. The poem that may result from this impression may be so successful that the reader will be more impressed with the incident as it is portrayed through words than he would have been with the actual flight of the bird. This enhancement of vitality, according to Browning's Fra Lippo Lippi, is the purpose of art. But for Cummings, regardless of how successful this enhancement may be, there is nevertheless an inherent *failure.* The vitality of the bird in flight, the essence, the peculiar alive quality which relates the bird to the core impulses of universal motions and forces, is a mysterious and intangible noumenon which the Artist through the senses of the Man can dimly perceive but never wholly re-create.

Failure is related to what Cummings has called the artist's "awful responsibility." The word suggests something of the depth of awe and humility that confronts the artist-poet when he glimpses through his art the world of *nothing*— that is, the order, harmony, and spiritual beauty of that unseen and indefinable force which informs all living things. The Artist-Man, even at the height of his artistic endeavor, at that moment when he kicks the three chairs out from under himself, is a *failure* because he cannot describe this living force. At best he can allude to its existence by revealing its occurrences in the tangible world. He cannot literally reproduce a bird, nor can he define in any exact manner the spirit that unites the bird to the harmony of the universe. The word *love* has connotations of this harmony. At best the poet brings his reader to a greater awareness of the existence of love. But ultimately he must fail: he cannot literally define what his vision conveys to him. In his sense of failure there is a humility that transcends all ego pretension, all self-aggrandizement at the expense of others. For Cummings, this is the individual: one who knows himself through love, a practitioner of love, that love which governs and harmonizes all life. This vision is not unlike Whitman's, who saw himself as a blade of grass, a microcosm of the selfsame spiritual force that governed the macrocosm. This awareness of self is sobering beyond the usual meaning of humility: it is more nearly akin to the artist's "awful responsibility."

Although Cummings also uses the word *nothing* in its most widely recognized meaning, his distinctive interpretation of the word appears throughout his poems. Consider the following extracts from a poem in *Tulips and Chimneys:*

> i have been sometimes true
> to Nothing and which lives
>
> .   .   .   .   .
>
> admitting i have been true
> only to the noise of worms.

Here, rather pointedly, Cummings is equating the concept of Nothing to the concept of being dead as a life force.

In a love poem from *is 5* ("some ask praise of their fellows"), he presents the argument that the poet or maker creates only in order to capture an essence of any particular of the lady's existence, and capture it truly.

> beyond these elements
>
> remarkably nothing is. . . .

Here again the emphasis placed upon the word *nothing*—note the stress the word receives through the syntactical arrangement of the line—connotes a spiritual existence beyond life and beyond all the gestures of the lady which represent life and love in its essence.

Or consider the implication of the word *nothing* in this progression from *XAIPE:*

> love,stand with me while silence sings
> not into nothing and nothing into never
> and never into(touch me!love)forever

Or in his volume *95 Poems* (Poem 30), notice the irony that adheres to the word *nothing* when the "him" being described finally discovers that the values he had projected in some tangible shape turn out to be "Less Than Nothing," and this "him" is left with the only real value that existed in the first place: "nothing."

> what Got him was Noth
>
> ing & nothing's exAct
> ly what any

one Living(or some
body Dead
like
even a Poet)could
hardly express what
i Mean is
what knocked him over Wasn't
(for instance)the Knowing your

whole(yes god

damned)life is a Flop or even
to
Feel how
Everything(dreamed
& hoped &
prayed for
months & weeks & days & years
& nights &
forever)is Less Than
Nothing(which would have been

Something)what got him was nothing

From *Tulips and Chimneys* through the last collection (*73 Poems*), *nothing* has continued to figure as a key word in Cummings' poetry. Poem 13 from *73 Poems* begins:

o
nly this
darkness(in
whom always i
do nothing) . . .

Perhaps the most explicit statement equating the artist (poet) with the achievement of *nothing* through recogni-

tion of self (the triumvirate of Artist-Man-Failure), occurs
in the elegy Cummings wrote to his mother (in *W* [*ViVa*]).
In tribute to his mother, Cummings indicates the love his
father felt for her:

> my father will be(deep like a rose
> tall like a rose)
>
> standing near my
>
> (swaying over her
> silent)
> with eyes which are really petals and see
>
> nothing with the face of a poet really which
> is a flower . . .

The eyes of the poet see *nothing*. Not only does the word
again indicate the concept of fulfillment, or the perpetuation of life through death, but it relates itself well to Cummings' idea of the poet's place in society. The poet, by being
nothing or seeing nothing, aligns himself with no causes,
no institutions, no saving ideas, etc.; he is free to observe
and exist, that is, free to cultivate himself. By being alone
and nothing, the poet can distinguish action from existence,
doing from being; action, or doing, is perhaps *the* method
of glossing over the terror of existence, of not having to
perceive or be aware of human finality. But the poet, by
being nothing in society, by cultivating himself, is alone
with such basic phenomena as stars, twilight, the moon, and
(in this particular poem) flowers, which all serve as symbols of a cycle of growth and love. Moreover, these phenomena renew themselves, and to this extent they are in
accord with the universal will of creation. Ironically, they

are so taken for granted, so constantly before us, that they are perceived as nothing in the usual sense of the word—devoid of significance. But to the poet they speak completeness, fulfillment, and rebirth—the ultimate of *nothing*.

For Cummings, then, the word *nothing* implies the "awful responsibility" the artist assumes, knowing he will fail. Finally, *nothing* is the ultimate goal of the Artist-Man-Failure, who in order to attain it must of necessity maintain fidelity to himself.

2. Subjects and Images

in China . . . Where a painter is a poet.
—from Cummings' foreword to the catalog
of an exhibition of his paintings, 1945

In *i:six nonlectures*, Cummings discussed the subject matter of his poetry in these terms: "as surely as each November has its April, mysteries only are significant; . . ." And again: ". . . I affirmed that—for me—personality is a mystery; that mysteries alone are significant; and that love is the mystery-of-mysteries who creates them all." Mysteries may here be defined as those aspects or natural phenomena of life capable of being perceived through the senses but incapable of being labeled or measured. In writing a poem Cummings stipulated one essential: that he concern himself with the unknown, immeasurable quintessence of his subject—the mystery.

Consider a man. He may be defined in the sports columns of a newspaper by his height, weight, speed; he may be described in sociological works in terms of the clothes he wears and the amount of money he possesses or spends; he may be analyzed in a chemistry text as a composite of various chemical ingredients in specified percentages; as a case in a psychology book he may be pronounced any one of a startling number of ists, phrenics, phobes, or various combinations thereof. With none of these categorical definitions is the poet concerned, for none constitutes the significance of the individual.

Categorical definitions of man were deplored by Emerson well over one hundred years ago. In his essay "The American Scholar" he tells us that ideally "there is One Man. . . . Man is not a farmer, or a professor, or an engineer, but he is all." Emerson writes that "the state of society is one in which the members have suffered amputation from the trunk, and strut about so many walking monsters—a good finger, a neck, a stomach, an elbow, but never a man. . . . The priest becomes a form; the attorney a statute book; the mechanic a machine; the sailor a rope of a ship." This tendency toward categorical definitions has gone much further in our present society.

Cummings is concerned with the whole man, and in writing a poem he attempts to make the poem become the man. That is, he attempts to portray for his readers that image of man which is splendid rather than sordid, magnanimous rather than petty. In short, Cummings presents an image of man in relation to his natural environment which no sets of facts can ever adequately define—as in the poem (from *no thanks*) that begins:

> conceive a man,should he have anything
> would give a little more than it away

Cummings feels that the essential dignity and nobility of man can remain intact in the city as well as in the country. And he has damned those forces that have reduced man to a cipher. Consider, for example, Poem 30 from *73 Poems*.

one winter afternoon

(at the magical hour
when is becomes if)

a bespangled clown
standing on eighth street
handed me a flower.

Nobody,it's safe
to say,observed him but

myself;and why?because

without any doubt he was
whatever(first and last)

mostpeople fear most:
a mystery for which i've
no word except alive

—that is,completely alert
and miraculously whole;

with not merely a mind and a heart

but unquestionably a soul—
by no means funereally hilarious

(or otherwise democratic)
but essentially poetic
or ethereally serious:

a fine not a coarse clown
(no mob,but a person)

and while never saying a word

who was anything but dumb;
since the silence of him

self sang like a bird.
Mostpeople have been heard
screaming for international

measures that render hell rational
—i thank heaven somebody's crazy

enough to give me a daisy

So far as Cummings is concerned, any perceivable incident or scene is poetic grist. Indeed, the array of subjects (from grasshoppers to Christmas trees, from barber poles to shooting stars) that confronts the casual reader of his poetry is startling.

In reading Cummings' poetry, then, it is helpful to know that he differs from most of his contemporaries in two basic ways: in his general attitude toward life, and in his method of employing subjects and images. His attitude toward existence largely informs and controls his poetic methods. The substance of it may be discovered, Cummings tells us (in the Introduction to *Collected Poems*), by noting the difference between the individual who is alive and "mostpeople" who are "snobs."

you and I are not snobs. We can never be born enough. We are human beings;for whom birth is a supremely welcome mystery,the mystery of growing:the mystery which happens only and whenever we are faithful to ourselves. You and I wear the dangerous looseness of doom and find it becoming. Life,for eternal us,is now;and now is much too busy being a little more than everything to seem anything,catastrophic included.

Cummings finds illimitable joy in everything truly alive. He turns an oftentimes brilliant and vitriolic satire upon those people who do not respond to life and upon the conventions, institutions, and beliefs with which they surround themselves to avoid or disguise reality.

Because of this basic attitude his poems often take on a radical appearance on the page. Subjects are presented for the simple purpose of calling attention to the properties of their vitality or for the purpose of dispelling set notions or beliefs about them. Hence poems such as the following, from *no thanks,* either intrigue readers with the ingenuity of their technique or cause them to decide that Cummings is writing in a private language to please only himself and perhaps the esoteric few.

                    r-p-o-p-h-e-s-s-a-g-r
                who
    a)s w(e loo)k
    upnowgath
            PPEGORHRASS
                            eringint(o-
    aThe):l
            eA
                !p:
    S   a
                (r
    rIvInG   .gRrEaPsPhOs)
                                        to
    rea(be)rran(com)gi(e)ngly
    ,grasshopper;

Through the spacings of word and letter and the use of capitals, the poet attempts to simulate the responses, particularly the auditory and visual responses, to the leap of a grasshopper from one point to another. When the grasshopper is in motion or when we see him only out of the corner of our eye, we cannot be sure of his identity; for this reason the letters of the word are jumbled until the end of the poem, when the grasshopper has come to rest, is still, and can be clearly seen for what it is. Other devices used to simulate visual response may be found in the descending, staggered printing of the word *leaps* to indicate the initial spring of the grasshopper, and in the spacing between the letter *S* of the word *leaps* and the letter *a* of the word *arriving* to suggest the arc or total distance of the leap. The capital letters of "PPEGORHRASS" are designed to suggest to the auditory sense the dry rattle of the grasshopper's wings in flight. In the penultimate line the parenthetical interruptions slow the tempo of the reading in such a way as to correspond to the gradual coalescing of impressions which confirm that the object of our immediate attention is a grasshopper.

Less radical in its appearance on the page is the poem below (Poem 48, *73 Poems*); yet like the one above this poem strives to fix our attention upon a simple incident or scene. Heightened awareness of this seemingly insignificant scene leads to a new dimension of understanding about existence, achieved not through mental but through sensory apprehension.

t,h;r:u;s,h;e:s

are
silent
now

.in silverly

notqu
-it-
eness

dre(is)ams

a
the
o

f moon

Part of the explanation for the syntax of this poem lies in Cummings' penchant for visual balance—the alternation of one- and three-line stanzas and the effect this achieves by posing a single line at the beginning and end of the poem. Note that Cummings carries this effort further by balancing the number of letters in the first and third lines of the three-line stanzas. Thus the letters in the second stanza balance 3–5–3, in the fourth stanza 5–2–5, and in the sixth stanza 1–3–1. The hyphens around "-it-" and the parenthetical marks around "is" serve to emphasize the words. The emphasis shows the contrast between the abstract connotations of the two: *it,* a thing (inanimate); *is,* alive (being). All these visual balances are not simply willful or eccentric: on the contrary, they suggest an underlying harmony which the poem is attempting to portray.

The marks of punctuation in the first line have two purposes: (1) they make the reader ponder the word (the why of such odd typography) and then extend this pondering to the significance of the word. Thrushes. Cummings lets the reader do the work of forming the image. You ponder the word and in the process see the meaning of the word. Hence the punctuation is a device. The comma, semicolon, colon, semicolon, comma, semicolon, and colon all have their usual function—that of indicating a pause. "Pause for the sake of clarity," these marks of punctuation say—and you pause, and see the thrushes. The beauty of this punctuation is that Cummings is using a device of abstraction to enforce the concrete and tangible properties of a word which the reader would normally glance over and understand—but not see. Irony is inherent in this device. Cummings is forcing almost meaningless abstractions back into the realm of vital significance. (2) There is a visual connotation in the punctuation. It asks you to see the thrushes on a branch of a tree or bush, clustered perhaps, but at any rate spaced as separate little beings (just as the letters of the word are spaced by the punctuation)—all perched and settled for their night's sleep.

The single period prominently placed at the beginning of line 5 suggests that the first four lines of the poem are also the last four lines. That is, one reading of the poem begins with the line ".in silverly"; the other reading begins with the first line.

The time of the poem is shortly after twilight when the atmosphere of the moon suggests a *notquite silverlyness,* when the thrushes "are . . . in silverly . . . dreams." This interpretation implies the ambiguity that Cummings' syntax enforces. All the visual balances mentioned above reinforce the so-called "meaning" of the poem. The period before "in silverly" establishes the structural ambiguity of the poem, which in turn compels the reader to see totality where before he had seen only division. That is to say, the poem gyres in upon itself to new dimensions of awareness by calling attention through syntax and typography to the moon and the thrushes as *one* essence, though they are apparently *two* things.

Notice how the poem may be read, thanks to Cummings' artistry. "t,h;r:u;s,h;e:s/ are/ silent/ now"—it is true. They have gone to bed. What is at all unusual about that? At this point we are on the blasé level of function which the workaday, routine, mechanized world requires of us. But then we are stopped by the period and the greater complexity of the remainder of the poem. We are asked to consider the thrushes in relation to their setting and hence in a dimension larger than that of the prosaic fact that they "are silent now." One of Cummings' miracles takes place before our eyes. We see that "in silverly notquiteness (is) a dream of the moon." What is that dream? The "t,h;r:u;s,h;e:s/ are." They "are . . . ams." The thrushes are a dream of the moon. The moon is a dream of the thrushes. The syntax forces this double interpretation to a single awareness— that the moon and the thrushes beautifully complement each other, that the moon takes its being from the thrushes, the thrushes their being from the moon. The two objects of the poem, the moon and the thrushes, coalesce spiritually into one.

The apparent scrambling of letters and words in the final stanzas is deliberate: it allows us to read the words around "dreams"

> is a dream
> are . . . dreams
> in . . . dreams
> dreams . . . of

as happening simultaneously in a grammatical sense. No word describes the process: elliptical ambiguity falters toward what is taking place around the word "dre(is)ams" but falls short of being an adequate description. But the consequences of this ordering of word and letter are there to be observed. Cummings' poems strive to show the spiritual affinity between objects which are apparently disparate. This poem thus becomes a metaphor for a way of life, for a way of being alive: to see the spiritual relatedness of things. Through syntax and typography, splintered vision is made whole.

The external shape of these poems is quite unlike that of most poems. Moreover, they differ radically from other poems (including a majority of Cummings' poems) in that they are apparently comments on a grasshopper and thrushes and nothing else. The relationship established between their subjects and the reader is immediate; the poems attempt to become the things they describe; they attempt to increase awareness by capturing some essence of existence that makes them alive and vital. The attitude in which the reader is asked to participate is akin to that of a child exploring with wonder a new-found world; each object perceived becomes the subject of rapt contemplation, an object wonderful and inspiring in itself, a marvel of creation.

The method of these poems could be related to that of the Imagists and those who purportedly were attempting to write what is now known as "pure poetry." The Imagists did not wholly succeed in their endeavor; nor do all of the poems of Cummings in this vein wholly succeed. In all such attempts an element of failure is inherent because it is apparently impossible for the mind of man to disassociate any object from some kind of mental classification. Thus, for example, one might put under the general category of *dangerous* such disparate phenomena as a roaring lion, high-voltage electric current, and a bear trap. This classifying tendency of man, however, in no way invalidates the attempt of the poet to restore the original freshness of his subject. On the contrary, Cummings asserts the responsibility of the poet to reinvest incidents and phenomena of life with their essential mystery, which alone is significant.

What is remarkable is the extent to which Cummings did succeed in writing poems about objects and incidents without external references. His use of subject matter is the reverse of standard practice. Where other poets begin with an idea (or perhaps a general conviction or awareness) which they exemplify with subjects and images—a process which T. S. Eliot has termed the discovery of an "objective correlative"—Cummings often begins with and goes no further than the subject or incident itself, assuming that the subject, seen for itself, will reveal its inherent significance. Here we have two polarities of method which, when effectively employed, converge upon very similar results. With Cummings, however, it is important to recognize how his method differs from conventional practice, as an aid to understanding his poetry.

Cummings does not present a system of thought; instead he presents a response to life. His statements express this response; his subjects and images embody it. They do not stand for something outside the poem (they are not symbols in the true sense of the word), but represent only themselves, as possessing life and vitality or not possessing it. They may be thought of as symbols only in relation to Cummings' statement that life is a mystery, an unknown quantity, and that in order to be alive one must constantly be aware of this fact.

Cummings' major subjects are love, birth, growth, dying, and their antitheses. (In his later poems he made a distinction between dying and death that will be discussed in its proper sequence.) Given his convictions about what constitutes value in life, these subjects are most appropriate; for they remain largely unknown (mysterious). It may even be that the poet alone (or a person of poetic temperament) has anything to say about them that is interesting or exciting.

For Cummings love is all-inclusive. In his opinion the effects of love are so widespread, from sensual and physical delight to life-giving force and life-perpetuating awareness, that many of his love poems are invested with wonder. This range of tone, from exuberance to awe, may easily be seen. Compare "her/flesh/Came" (from & [AND]) with "love is the every only god" (from *50 Poems*). The witty simile of the first provides humor. The latter is reverential.

Cummings' love poems are often addressed to the beloved; less often they are merely comments upon love. His basic thesis is that only those who are in love are alive and in harmony with the universe; that lack of love accounts for every misinterpretation of life. "Undead" and "notalive" are those who deny love, for they submit to the tyranny of convention and conformity which are sterilizers of the immediate response, which impose rules and ideas of propriety having nothing to do with love as it is felt, and which succeed only in distorting life. The poem "a man who had

fallen among thieves" (from *is 5*) illustrates the loveless
theory that once a man has been rolled you might as well
let him lie. Without his money he is worthless—Cummings'
modern version of the story of the Good Samaritan. But
Cummings' poem is also a parable of the contemporary
scene. The lack of human concern for the plight of a fellow
man is as prevalent as ever. The "thieves," however, are not
literally bandits or outlaws; they are rather those stultifying
forces of our society that have deprived the fallen man of
his soul and his integrity. Concern for the plight of the depraved is centered (now as always) in an individual who is
capable of love (the poet, perhaps), one who senses the
terror of the world of which the man who has succumbed
is a product.

One of Cummings' finest poems (from *50 Poems*) makes
explicit the difference between being in love and not being
in love.

> anyone lived in a pretty how town
> (with up so floating many bells down)
> spring summer autumn winter
> he sang his didn't he danced his did.
>
> Women and men(both little and small)
> cared for anyone not at all
> they sowed their isn't they reaped their same
> sun moon stars rain
>
> children guessed(but only a few
> and down they forgot as up they grew
> autumn winter spring summer)
> that noone loved him more by more

when by now and tree by leaf
she laughed his joy she cried his grief
bird by snow and stir by still
anyone's any was all to her

someones married their everyones
laughed their cryings and did their dance
(sleep wake hope and then) they
said their nevers they slept their dream

stars rain sun moon
(and only the snow can begin to explain
how children are apt to forget to remember
with up so floating many bells down)

one day anyone died i guess
(and noone stooped to kiss his face)
busy folk buried them side by side
little by little and was by was

all by all and deep by deep
and more by more they dream their sleep
noone and anyone earth by april
wish by spirit and if by yes.

Women and men (both dong and ding)
summer autumn winter spring
reaped their sowing and went their came
sun moon stars rain

This poem demonstrates Cummings' ability to give an abstract word concrete significance. He does this by placing the word in a syntax that allows it to retain its abstract meaning and at the same time take on a definite function. For example, in the opening line the indefinite pronoun *anyone* and the adverb *how* function in this dual capacity.

The word *anyone,* besides carrying its usual general meaning of referring to nobody in particular (or to some person who is in no way distinct or distinguished), is the appellation of a specific and highly individualistic person who is indeed distinguished. To his fellow townsmen he is just anyone; but to the reader of the poem who accepts its implicit values, he is that specific anyone who is capable of love. The word *how,* due to its syntactical position (an inversion of "how pretty"), is also enriched beyond its usual abstract properties of degree or manner. As an adjective modifying *town,* it is a superbly descriptive word suggesting in one touch the typical town where all values must conform to accepted regulations, decorum, and procedures, a town whose people operate on rigid and mechanical formalities: a "how town." With these two highly charged abstract words Cummings establishes in the opening line of his poem two opposed responses to life; the remainder of the poem dramatically juxtaposes these responses.

The poem celebrates the love of "anyone" and "noone" whose responses to life are in accord with the cyclic forces of the universe as evidenced by the seasonal changes of "spring summer autumn winter" and the majestic phenomena of "sun moon stars rain." Posed against the embracing love of "anyone" and "noone" are the routine existences of "women and men," the "someones," the "everyones," and "busy folk." "Anyone's" response to life was singing and dancing, positive expressions of exuberance and joy, but the activities of "women and men" were sowing and reaping—functional and routine behavior. Ironically, what these people sow and reap is negative sterility—"their isn't." Their existence after death will be as negative as it was

before death ("reaped their sowing and went their came").
But since their response to the manifestations of life ("tree
by leaf . . . bird by snow"), has always been positive,
"anyone" and "noone" will find in death a continuation of
that spiritual harmony they knew while alive—"wish by
spirit." More than this, since "anyone" and "noone" never
put limits upon their love or their responses to life, the
caution and circumspection and doubts about life enter-
tained by "women and men" and portrayed by the single
word *if* does not apply to "anyone" and "noone." Their
response to life has always been beyond "if" to "yes." Thus,
for these two lovers, there is no "if" about a perpetuating
existence. Their positive responses to life while alive insure
their spiritual inclusion in the forces of living after death—
"if by yes."

Growth, birth, and dying are manifestations of love, dependent upon love for their existence, and hence subsidiary
to love as a topic in Cummings' poems. One of Cummings'
most beautiful poems, "somewhere i have never travelled,
gladly beyond," from *W* (*ViVa*), integrates these topics.
Another poem from *no thanks,* "here's to opening and upward,to leaf and to sap," contrasts images of birth and
growth (in such words as "leaf" and "sap") with forces of
conformity and regulation (in such words as "must" and
"ought").

The following poem (from *50 Poems*) indicates, through
the parenthetical comment, that love is responsible for birth
and growth—that, in fact, love nurtures growth. The word
"memory" suggests love as a sustaining force, as a root is
the sustaining element of a young shoot or stem. The love

here described is that which gives but takes nothing, similar, perhaps, to the ideal love a mother would bear to a child.

> up into the silence the green
> silence with a white earth in it
>
> you will(kiss me)go
>
> out into the morning the young
> morning with a warm world in it
>
> (kiss me)you will go
>
> on into the sunlight the fine
> sunlight with a firm day in it
>
> you will go(kiss me
>
> down into your memory and
> a memory and memory
>
> i)kiss me(will go)

Against the common acceptance of death as a finality, Cummings poses the concept that dying is a natural extension of life. The love of "anyone" and "noone" for each other and for the simple phenomena of their world prepared them for inclusion in the spiritual realm of the universe. In this respect, then, dying (or the concept of death) is a part of the life cycle of birth, growth, and fulfillment. The place of death in this cycle is that of renewal or reintegration with the invisible essence that informs all living things. Through love the essence of life is experienced; consequently dying is recognized not as cessation but as integration with this informing essence. Throughout the body of Cummings' poetry examples may be found to illustrate this concept.

In this passage from *Tulips and Chimneys,* his first book of poetry, love and death are directly equated:

> Come hither
> O thou, is love not death?

In the poem "when god lets my body be" from the same volume, the continuation of the spirit of life after death is portrayed through a number of images of living objects in which, according to the speaker of the poem, his own being will be infused.

The final couplet in the last poem of the volume *XAIPE,* separated from *Tulips and Chimneys* by twenty-seven years, continues this paradox about death. The speaker of this poem regards the cyclical moon as evidence of birth, growth, fulfillment, and integration—visibly portrayed. He asks that the "secret" of reintegration (rebirth through death) be revealed to him.

> teach disappearing also me the keen
> illimitable secret of begin

Cummings persisted in this conviction. In the last poem of his last volume (*73 Poems*) he wrote:

> your lover(looking through both life and death)
> timelessly celebrates the merciful
>
> wonder no world deny may or believe

One final quotation (from *is 5*) shows the power of love extending through and beyond death to a re-entry into the essence of life.

> . . . Love
> coins His most gradual gesture,
>
> and whittles life to eternity

In his later poetry Cummings makes an interesting distinction between the terms *dying* and *death*. Where in his early and middle volumes of poetry Cummings seemed to use these two terms interchangeably, in his later collections of poems he assigns a specific value to each. The following poem from *XAIPE* is built upon this distinction between *dying* and *death*.

>   dying is fine)but Death
>
>   ?o
>   baby
>   i
>
>   wouldn't like
>
>   Death if Death
>   were
>   good:for
>
>   when(instead of stopping to think)you
>
>   begin to feel of it,dying
>   's miraculous
>   why?be
>
>   cause dying is
>
>   perfectly natural;perfectly
>   putting
>   it mildly lively(but
>
>   Death

is strictly
scientific
& artificial &

evil & legal)

we thank thee
god
almighty for dying

(forgive us,o life!the sin of Death

In one sense, the distinction that Cummings is making here is between a noun and a gerund. *Death* as a noun is a classification, and as we use the word today it takes on all the connotations of our highly sophisticated society; it is, as Cummings points out, "strictly/ scientific" with all the apparatus of the science of embalming; it is "artificial," not only in the finished product of the corpse after preparation by the embalmer, but also, perhaps, in the atmosphere of the funeral home and in the elaborate ritual of procession and service; it is "evil" in the sense that it is commonly thought of as a blight upon happiness, a great misfortune which shatters the illusion of security of those still breathing; and, finally, it is "legal."

Dying, on the other hand, suggests a movement, an invisible transformation or change of condition that man to no great extent has been able to alter or impede or ritualize or squeeze into a pattern of conformity. *Dying,* as Cummings notes, "is/ perfectly natural": man has not yet succeeded in disguising it as something else. The superb irony of describing *dying* as "perfectly/ putting/ it mildly lively" cannot be missed. Thus we see that dying is an extension of life; for the individual who responds with love to the phenomena of his existence, it is ultimate communion with the mystery of life; it is integration with the invisible universal force that impels birth and growth; in short, it is "lively."

To his basic subjects of love, growth, birth, and dying Cummings brought a number of images that for him represent beauty and vitality. Beauty for Cummings resides for the most part in the natural scene, urban or rural, particularly in the muted light of sunset or dusk when impressions of objects are intensified and brought into sharp relief. The mystery of twilight compels awe and wonder; the mood of a twilight poem is often one of revery and dream; the primary urge is toward love, perhaps because the sense of loneliness is greater than at any other time. And all objects that in themselves are described as appealing in form or motion take on an additional grace and mystery of shape in the aura of the setting sun as in these two excerpts, from poems in *&:*

> my naked lady framed
> in twilight is an accident
>
> whose niceness betters easily the intent
> of genius—
>   painting wholly feels ashamed
> before this music, and poetry cannot
> go near because perfectly fearful.

> Paris; this April sunset completely utters
> utters serenely silently a cathedral

before whose upward lean magnificent face
the streets turn young with rain,

spiral acres of bloated rose
coiled within cobalt miles of sky
yield to and heed
the mauve
                of twilight(who slenderly descends,
daintily carrying in her eyes the dangerous first stars)

These are but two examples taken from a number that could have been used equally well. For Cummings, sunset and twilight playing upon various objects and landscapes produces a powerful impression and is perhaps the most dominant image in his poetry.

Another very prominent image throughout Cummings' poetry is that of flowers—particularly roses. Although flowers are often equated with the human face and flower petals with human lips, their general significance is that of natural growth and beauty responding in love to rain and sunlight. Cummings' only prose comment on flowers may be found in *EIMI:* "(K)there is an I Feel;an actual universe or alive of which our merely real world or thinking existence is at best a bad,at worst a murderous,mistranslation;flowers give me this actual universe." In a general way, this same comment could be applied to all of Cummings' major images, which represent a positive response to life.

Besides twilight and flowers the most important images in Cummings' poetry are the moon, stars, mountains, the ocean, snow, wind, rain, sunlight and the sun, dawn, birds, trees, buds, leaves, the sky, and children. Spring, as a marvel of growth and life, is eulogized in many of Cummings' poems. These images taken as a group represent for Cummings the external manifestation of the immeasurable, life-promoting force that infuses the universe. To disregard the truth of life as represented by these images is to exist in a kind of self-inflicted hell where the beliefs that are thought to be real are only vagaries and illusions of the mind.

Although Cummings sometimes combines or associates as many as four or five of these images in one poem, probably nowhere do so many of them come together as in what has been entitled "Speech (From a Forthcoming Play)," published in 1936 in *The New American Caravan*. The speech is a prophecy indicating that the rebirth of the world, as the result of an apparently self-inflicted cataclysmic destruction, will depend upon a recognition of these images as the true purveyors of life. Part of the speech, showing the importance that Cummings attaches to these images, follows:

Don't worry; don't try to imagine, the stars know; and the trees even when bursting with buds, sometimes if bending under snow. Wave your voice, make people die, hide in the nonexistence of an atom, get the garbage concession tovarich—that makes no difference; only flowers understand. O little, O most very little civilization, pull your eyes in and kiss all your beautiful machines goodnight; yesterday was another day, which doesn't matter— roses are roses. I swear to you by my immortal head: if sunsets are magnificent (though leaves fall, smiles pass) there shall arrive a whisper—but after the whisper, wonder; and next, death; then laughter (O, all the world will laugh—you never smelled such a world): finally, beginning; a bird beyond every bird, oceans young like mountains, universe absurdly beyond opening universe opening, freedom, function of impossibility, the philo-psycho-socialistico-losophers curl up; you die, I melt —only we may happen, suddenly who by disappearing perfectly into destiny are fatally alive. Be alive therefore; generously explode and be born, be like the sea, resemble mountains, dance; it shall not be forgiven you—open your soul as if it were a window and with a not visible cry bravely (through this immeasurable intensely how silent yesterday) fall upon the skilful thunderously and small awful unmeaning and the joy and upon the new inexcusably tomorrowing immensity of flowers.

It may be said of Cummings that, unlike many of his contemporaries, he recognizes a system of value still in existence in the universe. Part of this recognition stems from his own inheritance (his childhood home, his experience of parental love, etc.), and part of it from his own assiduous cultivation of what he believes to be the truth about being alive. What apparently saved Cummings from the feelings of despair and futility that afflicted so many intelligent people during the first three or four decades of the century, is the fact that his creed of living in no way depended upon even a tacit acceptance of ideologies inherited from the nineteenth century except perhaps the broader assumptions of transcendentalism and the romantic appeal to nature. Certainly scientific progress, the traditional forms of religion, and political and economic ideologies had no place in Cummings' scheme of values. Hence when the debacles of our century (war, depression, and the shiftings of political power) drove a great many thinking people into skepticism and despair, Cummings, who had never placed trust or hope in stereotyped beliefs in the first place, remained free to mock or jeer or sing the praises of growth and love— and it is just this aspect of freshness and the inviolability of self in the face of preponderant gloom over the loss of futile beliefs that is undoubtedly his greatest appeal for most of his readers. Thus, when most poets were writing about April being a cruel month in one way or another, Cummings was enthusiastically embracing the joy of spring "when the world is mud-/ luscious. . . ." And when other poets were cataloguing the desolation of spirit and the prevalence of death, Cummings was lyrically proclaiming that for the man whose heart was intact there was still much to jest about, laugh at, or respond to. He begins one of his sonnets (from *1 × 1*): "life is more true than reason will deceive." He concludes another (from "New Poems" in *Collected Poems*) with: "I'd rather learn from one bird how to sing/ than teach ten thousand stars how not to dance." Cummings can identify the images of sterility, but his favorite images convey vitality.

3. Freedom and the Individual

the single secret will still be man
—*1 × 1,* 20

From the Age of Enlightenment we have inherited the notion that reason is an infallible guide in human affairs. But Cummings has written (in *no thanks*): "reason let others give and realness bring—/ ask the always impossible of me." Today we are as much convinced as were our eighteenth-century forefathers that "hard, clear thinking" alone will solve our problems, both national and international. Cummings made a gnomic statement that is reprinted in "nonlecture four" of *i:six nonlectures;* it reads: "think twice before you think." In *EIMI* he has summarily stated: "down with thinking. Vive feeling!" And again in *EIMI* he writes: "Not to completely feel is thinking. May I be allowed to feel,if you please?"

The poems continue the evidence of the prose in revealing Cummings' opinion of the danger of thinking and not feeling. In a satirical poem (in *no thanks*) he has written: "he does not have to feel because he thinks/ (the thoughts of others,be it understood)." One poem in *&* begins: "let's live suddenly without thinking/ under honest trees." The first stanza of a poem in *is 5* reads:

> since feeling is first
> who pays any attention
> to the syntax of things
> will never wholly kiss you;

Poem 89 of *95 Poems* contains a parenthetical comment of no uncertain meaning: "(exists no/ miracle mightier than this:to feel)." Poems 35 and 62 of Cummings' last volume (*73 Poems*) reiterate his position. The latter poem goes a step further and in this excerpt implies that the thinking process is finite and futile.

> hide,poor dishonoured mind
> who thought yourself so wise;
> and much could understand
> concerning no and yes:

It should come as no surprise that Cummings' attitude toward the thinking process in its usual manifestations— along with his corollary belief in the primacy of the indi- vidual—has excited criticism. He has been termed a "ro- mantic anarchist," a "solipsist," a "nihilist," and a member of an "anti-culture group." [1] Another charge is that the

---

[1] See F. O. Matthiessen, "Four American Poets," in *The Responsibili- ties of the Critic* (New York: Oxford University Press, 1952), pp. 119,

tragic aspect of human existence is missing from his poems and as a result the joy of living he does celebrate is immature and childish.[2] His love poems, we are told, are "neo-primitive" and without "complication or pain or moral significance." [3] In the opinion of one critic, Cummings "crowds other individuals off stage, . . . rejects other ideas in the name of his own integrity, . . . prepares endlessly for self-affirmation by endlessly discarding and rejecting the work of others." [4] This same critic states that the people about whom the poet writes are one-dimensional representatives of either the affirmative or negative approach to life, that as such they are presented as caricatures with no indication of how "they think or feel." [5] Cummings' attitude, according to one observer, does not bring reality into sharper focus, but instead distorts "his perception of the outer world." [6] In a wholesale attack one writer asserts that his poetry preaches a "nihilism"; that his concept of love depends upon sex alone for its expression; that women seem to be of value only as they are physically attractive; and that the individualism the poet champions is undemocratic in nature.[7] But the charge most often repeated by critics is

---

120; Eleanor M. Sickels, "The Unworld of E. E. Cummings," *American Literature,* XXVI (May, 1954), 223; R. P. Blackmur, "Notes on E. E. Cummings' Language," *The Hound and the Horn,* IV (Jan.–Mar., 1931), 164.

[2] Sickels, p. 237; Randall Jarrell, "The Profession of Poetry," *Partisan Review,* XVII (September, 1950), 730.

[3] Jarrell, p. 729.

[4] Robert M. Adams, "grasshopper's waltz: the poetry of e. e. cummings," *Cronos,* I (Fall, 1947), 5.

[5] *Ibid.*

[6] John Finch, "New England Prodigal," *New England Quarterly,* XII (December, 1939), 647–648.

[7] Sickels, pp. 223–227.

that his poetry has shown no development or growth in scope and significance.[8]

Against a poet who seemed to hold thinking processes suspect, these indictments would seem easy enough to substantiate. But Cummings thought—as all of us do—and better than most of us. He thought about what most of us think (or think we think) about; and he thought about what he felt. Where many of us think in terms of good or bad, right or wrong, true or false, stop or go, Cummings thought in terms of curiosity, wonder, and exploration. He met life with an open heart and a mind attuned to sensory impressions and feelings. What do I feel? What is my feeling response? These are the important questions for Cummings and his criteria for being alive. He used his mind to reflect on his personal involvement with things he experienced, and as a consequence was able to distinguish beautifully between what he felt inwardly and what he felt outwardly—that is, what he felt in himself and what he felt toward things outside himself. This kind of dual awareness is apparently rare and possibly an art. It is the basis of Cummings' interpretation of what it is that constitutes reality and what it means to be alive. It is the crux of his vision. It explains the paradoxical turn of his attitudes and opinions. Obviously Cummings used his mind to think. As a practicing poet he made countless thinking choices. (He told me that he worked on one of his poems over a span of ten years.) But he denied the supremacy of the mind over the heart, of thinking over feeling. He trusted himself to interpret his feelings for the truth of his existence.

[8] Matthiessen, p. 119; Adams, p. 6; Jarrell, p. 729; James G. Southworth, "E. E. Cummings," *Some Modern American Poets* (Oxford: Bassil Blackwell, 1950), p. 135.

Although he occasionally called himself a "nonhero," the meaning Cummings attaches to two key terms in his lexicon—*freedom* and *individual*—is much more apropos to his stance as a member of society and his vision as a poet. In this chapter I hope to develop a perceptive understanding of what he meant by these terms. About individuals he had this to say in a sonnet from *50 Poems.*

> there are possibly 2½ or impossibly 3
> individuals every several fat
> thousand years. Expecting more would be
> neither fantastic nor pathological but
>
> dumb. . . .

In this same sonnet Cummings refers to Christ as "Him Whose blood was for us spilled." For Cummings, Christ was a supreme individual who, responsible to himself and totally assured of his own dignity, was capable of extending love and granting dignity to other human beings. In fact, all of Cummings' individuals, from the bum who picks up old cigarette butts or "dominic" the "icecoalwood" man to Ford Madox Ford or Aristide Maillol or even Santa Claus—all possess and extend dignity. None of them are solipsists or nihilists by any definition of these words. Rather, like the kingbird, as Cummings tells us in Poem 2 of *73 Poems,* they know their worth in relation to those whom they love.

> for any ruffian of the sky
> your kingbird doesn't give a damn—
> his royal warcry is I AM
> and he's the soul of chivalry

.   .   .   .   .

true to his mate his chicks his friends
he loves because he cannot fear

Freedom, of course, is a slippery word, difficult to define. Cummings emphasized the absence of mental restrictions of any kind. The fact that a man can come and go or *do* as he pleases is no sign that he is free. Cummings believed that a man is free when he is allowed to *be* himself. He believed that a man can be himself only when he is not shackled to creed, beliefs, dogma, ideologies. When Cummings got out of Russia, he wrote in *EIMI:* ". . . and I also am LAUGHING!actually can you imagine at ideas at ideals at ideology at anything which would corrupt the natural pervert the distinct poison the eternal warp the incorruptible. . . ." A man can be himself by reflecting on his responses and feeling awarenesses. If he accepts the truth he senses, he is free. If, however, he lives by the creeds and slogans he has been taught to believe, he is not free. One of the foremost attributes of the individual is that he resists the tyranny of thinking and practices the freedom of feeling alive.

In his freedom the individual retains the right, always, to decline making a choice between mental alternatives or hypothetical distinctions. A feeling response is immediate and spontaneous: mental choice is ponderous and considered. It may be that there is no such thing as choice in life: we only think there is, for the choices and decisions we make are always within finite contexts that we think we understand, whereas in truth the great generative and degenerative forces in the universe go on in spite of our puny efforts to slow them or speed them. As a consequence of this realization, the individual is concerned with miracles, mysteries, and the unknown. "Life,for eternal us,is now" Cummings wrote in the 1938 Introduction to *Collected Poems*. Why now? Because inherent in the now is the mystery of life and growth and the awareness of being alive, which is why Cummings said in this same Introduction: "You and I wear the dangerous looseness of doom and find it becoming." That is to say, we know that we are alive because we are aware that we are involved in the process of dying, one of the great mysteries.

What has this view of life got to do with the concept of choice? Nothing, obviously: choice is nonexistent. You choose death no more than you choose life. Suicide is simply an uncreative act. The individual, however, embraces the unknown—and life has as much to discover as death. Trees, for example, are to climb, not classify in some way. Those who do not dare for fear of falling, know nothing about "the dangerous looseness of doom." Fall if you must—that's being alive. In *The Enormous Room,* after The Imp has fallen from the tallest tree in the prison yard, his father The Wanderer picks him up and says: " 'Don't be sad, my little son, everybody falls out of trees, they're made for that by God. . . .' "

In this same book Cummings is faced with a situation that illustrates superbly what freedom means for the individual. Men who are not free think of choice as a necessity. They think it entails making a decision between one of two or more methods, ideas, or systems of thought. When Cummings was confronted with the alternative of professing hatred for the entire German nation or being classified as an enemy sympathizer, he declined to make a sophistic choice. That is, he chose not to choose between alternatives that offered no real choice. His allegiance was to himself, to the truth of his feelings—and his feelings were those of concern for his friend, Slater Brown, who had been unjustly imprisoned. Paradoxically, under these circumstances, prison meant freedom for Cummings. Here is the crisis scene.

'Est-ce-que vous detestez les boches?'
I had won my case. The question was purely perfunctory. To walk out of the room a free man I had merely to say yes. My examiners were sure of my answer. The rosette was leaning forward and smiling encouragingly. The moustache was making little *oui*'s in the air with his pen. And Noyon had given up all hope of making me out a criminal. I might be rash, but I was innocent; the dupe of a superior and malign intelligence. I would probably be admonished to choose my friends more carefully next time, and that would be all. . . .
Deliberately, I framed the answer:
'Non. J'aime beaucoup les français.'
Agile as a weasel, Monsieur le Ministre was on top of me: 'It is impossible to love Frenchmen and not to hate Germans.'
I did not mind his triumph in the least. The discomfiture of the rosette merely amused me. The surprise of the moustache I found very pleasant.
Poor rosette! He kept murmuring desperately: 'Fond of his friend, quite right. Mistaken of course, too bad, meant well.'

It takes no great perspicacity to see that the logic of the examiners is specious: love for Frenchmen is not equivalent to hate for Germans. Cummings chose to keep his integrity by declining to choose between alternatives that, for him, were neither valid nor appropriate. For the individual who is free, choice always includes the infinite perspective of no choice. Cummings had no choice in the matter. He did not detest Germans. For him being a "free man" meant having a free conscience. Consequently, he went to prison.

This incident has its epilogue in Cummings' poetry. For those who believe in classifications of right and wrong, the dilemma Cummings faced may seem very real. Cummings did not think so. For him the integrity of an individual is far more precious than belief in any of the superficial distinctions of good and bad contrived by the intellect of men in society. Thus in *1 × 1* he writes:

> dead every enormous piece
> of nonsense which itself must call
> a state submicroscopic is—
> compared with pitying terrible
> some alive individual

Cummings said that "mostpeople are snobs." The interesting thing about this remark is that the moment a person actively resents it, he is no longer a snob. If by snob we are referring to people who depend upon conventional and widespread opinion for their sense of security and upon acceptance by the group for their sense of status, then Cummings is right. An individual is *I* or *you*. A group is *we* or *they*. Anyone who talks in terms of *we* or *they* at the expense of *I* or *you* has lost his identity. Notice how Cummings (in *EIMI*) answers the questions of the interviewer for the Soviet Embassy.

Then you wish to go to Russia as a writer and painter? Is that it?

no;I wish to go as myself.

(An almost smile). Do you realize that to go as what you call Yourself will cost a great deal?

I've been told so.

Let me earnestly warn you(says the sandyhaired spokesman for the Soviet Embassy in Paris)that such is the case. Visiting Russia as you intend would be futile from every point of view. The best way for you to go would be as a member of some organization—

but,so far as I know,I'm not a member of any organization.

The situation is so familiar (or perhaps unfamiliar) that its import is overlooked; nevertheless, the threat to personal identity is continuous, pervasive, insidious. Cummings said that "You and I are human beings" because the words *You* and *I* refer to one person at a time. Too often people acting as a group lose the characteristics of a human being. They come to be governed by ideas, and ideas can be deadly. For example, you (reader, reading these words) are probably a member of a group called the United States of America, which for a number of years has been engaged in building the most awful weapons of total destruction the world has known. Behind this activity there is an idea about defense. In the glare of the destructive potential of these weapons, it becomes clear that the idea has no validity. Defense through total destruction is "enormous . . . nonsense." In Poem 38 of *XAIPE* we find these lines:

> . . . if the quote state unquote says
> "kill" killing is an act of christian love.

Here is one more example of the fallible mind taking prece-dence over the infallible heart which feels. The individual feels truth. He thinks about what he feels instead of feeling sick about what he thinks. For the individual, schemes and beliefs do not take precedence over the truth as it is intuitively felt. This is the great difference between what Cummings terms "You and I and mostpeople."

The charge that Cummings lacks insight into the tragic aspect of human existence needs clarification. If the calamitous is thought of as tragic, it can be safely said that Cummings saw all too well the forces that contribute to the sadness of things, to the heartache and misery of "mostpeople." He also saw that these forces are put into operation by the principles which govern human relations in our society—namely expediency and exploitation. He wrote in *Adventures in Value* that "muckers don morningcoats,masters become their servants' servants,thieves are acclaimed & liars applauded,unchildren murder their nonparents,& politicians inherit the earth." Man, he knew, is afflicted with his own worst instincts. In comparison with the woe man has wrought upon himself, he suffers to a negligible degree from natural disasters—earthquake, flood, famine. Rather his predicament is that of having to live with his own stupidity, foolishness, and lack of regard for human dignity. Man suffers from the inability or unwillingness to extend sympathy and consideration to others. War, disease, fear of old age and death, crime, destructive rivalry based upon greed, racial prejudice and its attendant horrors, poverty, class pretensions, and all the other grievances that cluster about man are the products of his own indigent nature and the ideologies he has designed to accommodate his behavior and his wants in terms of greed, suspicion, fear, and hate. The individuals of the world have tried without success to con-

vince man that he may know others by knowing himself,
accord the respect and dignity to others that he expects for
himself. Unfortunately, man is a slow learner, as Cummings
observed in this poem from *1 × 1*.

plato told

him:he couldn't
believe it(jesus

told him;he
wouldn't believe
it)lao

tsze
certainly told
him,and general
(yes

mam)
sherman;
and even
(believe it
or

not)you
told him:i told
him;we told him
(he didn't believe it,no

sir)it took
a nipponized bit of
the old sixth

avenue
el;in the top of his head:to tell

him

In the classic sense of the word, though, none of modern man's tribulations are tragic. Correspondingly, Cummings' poems are not tragic in the sense that the plays of Sophocles are tragic. The explanation for this lack is not difficult. A tragic hero is always involved with an idea about transgression, and out of deference to that idea thinks that he must act. As I have already noted, Cummings' "nonhero" individual holds ideas suspect and regards *doing* as no guarantee that the doer is alive to the possibilities of his existence. In addition, if choice is inoperative in Cummings' illimitable view of life, then the classic concept of tragedy, based as it is on choice between courses of action, would have no validity for the individual. In the Greek sense of the word Cummings' poems, it is true, contain nothing of the tragic.

Greek tragedy assumes the dignity of man. The tragedy of modern man is that he has lost his dignity. In our time tragedy stems not from man's failure to recognize and accept his limitations but from failure to realize his own unique identity and potentiality. He has lost his dignity not because he has laid claim to powers beyond his scope and ability but because he has relegated his rights and responsibilities to abstractions of government and society. Consequently, the need for people today to know themselves as individuals is desperate. The tragedy today is that people have crammed themselves into conformistic boxes of established mores, convictions, and beliefs about reality and correct behavior. The result is that they are able to relate to each other only as boxes of beliefs and ideas and not as individual human beings—and this is tragic. In Cummings' opinion, unless a person knows himself as an individual, he is unable to express himself, to say who he is. Instead he refers to an idea he thinks he believes or to his membership in a group. That is, he gives you information about the dimensions of his box but nothing about himself. Thus Cummings writes: " 'the tragedy of life always hasn't been and'(he added quietly)'isn't that some people are poor and others rich,some hungry and others not hungry,some weak and others strong. The tragedy is and always will be that most people are unable to express themselves.' " (*EIMI*).

Two conclusions rise from this definition of tragedy. The first is that the individual who can express himself will invariably not be understood by people who cannot; the result is an infinite loneliness which Cummings often compares to the plight of a star. Individuals suffer this loneliness, as do poets, as did Christ. From *XAIPE* comes this poem:

> no time ago
> or else a life
> walking in the dark
> i met christ
>
> jesus)my heart
> flopped over
> and lay still
> while he passed(as
>
> close as i'm to you
> yes closer
> made of nothing
> except loneliness

The other conclusion is that to cavil at Cummings for not treating man's existence as tragic is absurd. He sees the traditional view as inapplicable. But he does reveal the tragedy of modern man.

The individual offers a kaleidoscope of views but no final or conclusive definition. He derives vitality from a spontaneous and uninhibited response to natural manifestations of life. He is a lover, and love makes his loneliness tolerable. His instinct for self-preservation leads him to include others in his love, to impart to them the joy he finds in being alive. Although the full significance of the individual's love may at best be dimly perceived by others or by a particular beloved one, nevertheless it is finally his reason for being. It is the link between him and his fellow men, a mystery, a miracle.

. . . With you I leave a remembrance of miracles:they are by somebody who can love and who shall be continually reborn,a human being;somebody who said to those near him,when his fingers would not hold a brush "tie it into my hand"—(Introduction to *Collected Poems*)

Because every time you shift the perspective on the individual he offers another facet of interpretation, this chapter could go in a nondirectional way at some length. Before closing, however, I should like to present Cummings' definitive non-description of Zulu, from *The Enormous Room*. Those true individuals whom Cummings met he termed "Delectable Mountains" (after Bunyan's *Pilgrim's Progress*)—and Zulu was one of these.

There are certain things in which one is unable to believe for the simple reason that he never ceases to feel them. Things of this sort—things which are always inside of us and in fact are us and which consequently will not be pushed off or away where we can begin thinking about them—are no longer things; they, and the us which they are, equals A Verb; an IS. The Zulu, then, I must perforce call an IS.

In a much more succinct way, Cummings said in his Introduction to *Collected Poems* that the individual "is democracy." This statement strikes me as a flat rebuttal to the charge that his poetry preaches anarchy or denies the virtues of democracy—because what particularly distinguishes the individual is his humane vision. That is to say, the perspective of the individual comprises the ideal of democracy —freedom and a sense of personal integrity. Unfortunately, a society based upon codes of exploitation can only give lip service to this ideal. When men are thought of in terms of statistics, numbers, or manipulative digits and treated the same way, then there is a corresponding lack of that humane vision which regards them as human beings: feeling, sympathy, and the willingness to grant dignity and respect. But the individual sees through all the paraphernalia— knowledge, systematic diagnoses, and classifications—with which man surrounds himself in the attempt to identify himself and the world. The individual reaches straight through to the basic substance of humanity which characterizes all people, and for the length of time that he touches others they respond with a joy in life that they were unaware of possessing. Joy and dignity are inherent in the free man. But man, to be free, must realize that he himself is more important and more real than any ideal that limits or classifies him. To rescue his fellow men from the depravity of sterile abstractions is the responsibility of the individual.

It is a spontaneous manifestation of love upon which his own sense of dignity and freedom depends.

Numerous poems illustrate this relation of the individual to his fellow men. Some of them are statements; others refer to specific persons. Of these poems none, perhaps, is so well known as Cummings' eulogy of his father. Here is another—from *XAIPE:*

who sharpens every dull
here comes the only man
reminding with his bell
to disappear a sun

and out of houses pour
maids mothers widows wives
bringing this visitor
their very oldest lives

one pays him with a smile
another with a tear
some cannot pay at all
he never seems to care

he sharpens is to am
he sharpens say to sing
you'd almost cut your thumb
so right he sharpens wrong

and when their lives are keen
he throws the world a kiss
and slings his wheel upon
his back and off he goes

but we can hear him still
if now our sun is gone
reminding with his bell
to reappear a moon

In this poem the knife-sharpener, an individual, responds to other people directly with love and sympathy. He brings joy and vitality and he makes the lives of others keen. He comes and he goes with the same kind of simple majesty with which the sun and moon appear and disappear. In harmony with the universe, he would harmonize others, teach them the perception of a universal accord which includes all that is worthy of love in the human race.

As Cummings has said, the individual represents the ideal of democracy. He lives in freedom. True democracy requires that all its constituents be free and hence individuals. Such a society would consist of persons who through an awareness of and devotion to themselves are capable of granting to others an equal regard. In effect Cummings has postulated a selflessness based upon a reference to self, a spiritual accord and social unity achieved through individuality. For Cummings freedom and the individual are synonyms for democracy and love.

4. The Themes

children guessed(but only a few
and down they forgot as up they grew
— *50 Poems,* 29

Cummings' concept of the individual did not emerge fully
developed at the beginning of his career to be reaffirmed
through successive volumes of poetry without any percepti-
ble change or increase in significance, as has too often been
stated. Rather, the early volumes primarily celebrate the
simple joy of living through the senses, though they also
contain some of Cummings' best satiric pieces.

The middle volumes, beginning approximately with *is 5*
in 1926, reaching a culmination with *no thanks* in 1935,
and showing evidence of a changing emphasis with *50
Poems* in 1940, reveal a heightened and defensively sensitive
awareness of the individual in relation to his social environment. A noticeably larger number of poems are satiric in
tone; they expose specific incidents, occupations, and conventions in thought and behavior that in Cummings' view

threaten the individual perception. Poems of objective detail without overt statement now appear on occasion in the form of a pictogram or ideogram. Primarily, however, sensory perception during this middle period is used as a test or a contrast to reveal disparity between what the individual perceives as truth and what the intellect has inculcated. The statement in the middle poems is built upon the sensory awareness that informs the earlier poetry. In no way has faith in the immediate sensory perception diminished; rather the appeal to the senses, the human response, now has a broader purpose; it supports and adds weight to the critical vision of the individual examining social behavior.

With the publication of *50 Poems* another important dimension becomes evident in Cummings' poetry. Beginning approximately with this volume and extending through *95 Poems* in 1958 and *73 Poems* in 1963, we find Cummings examining the positive impact that the individual exerts upon his fellow men. As we have seen, what the individual has to offer, what the pattern of his life illustrates, is love. He is a practitioner of love for life, for others, and for one particular beloved. In the latest poems the individual emerges as the only true exponent of love. He is in harmony with himself and the world around him. He finds himself a microcosm of the cyclic harmony of the universe. In touch with the truth of his existence and serenely confident of human dignity, the individual affects others by stirring in them an awareness of joy, self-respect, and love. Cummings wrote that his father "woke dreamers to their ghostly roots." This role of the individual adds a new dimension to Cummings' themes; but nothing of major emphasis in the earlier poetry has been discarded. It is this integrated thematic unity that

has misled certain critics into assuming that Cummings'
poetry has shown neither growth nor change. The charge is
not just. Although Cummings' basic position has never
wavered, his poetry does reveal growth in perception and a
steady increase in depth and significance.

In his Introduction to a London reprint of *1 × 1*, Lloyd
Frankenberg said that, in effect, all of Cummings' poems
were "love poems." With equal truth it could be said that
all of the poems are based on the premise that we know
only what our senses tell us, or that all are presentments of
life through the individual perspective. These are the basic
themes of all of Cummings' writing. They are interdependent. Taken in the order Cummings has emphasized them in
his poetry, they may be listed as follows:

1. The primacy of sensory awareness (of feeling).
2. The integrity of the individual.
3. The realization of love.

In the order listed these themes point up Cummings' growth
as a poet.

The earliest poetry not only affirms that the senses are
the means by which life is revealed, but the poetry itself is
sensuous, replete with archaic terms suggesting romantic
distance and exotic images around which cluster vague emotions suggested through the connotative value of abstract
adjectives. Something of the ethereal, nebulous quality of
this early verse may be seen in the first stanza of the poem
entitled "Of Nicolette," from *Tulips and Chimneys*.

> dreaming in marble all the castle lay
> like some gigantic ghost-flower born of night
> blossoming in white towers to the moon,

soft sighed the passionate darkness to the tune
of tiny troubadours, and (phantom-white)
dumb-blooming boughs let fall their glorious snows,
and the unearthly sweetness of a rose
swam upward from the troubled heart of May;

However, Cummings soon came to recognize that the simple presentation of sensual exuberance was not enough, that the value of a phenomenon resided in its inherent essence as revelation about the meaning of life. As a consequence a number of things occurred: the romantic imagery and setting were dropped along with archaic terms and the many allusions to myths and mythological figures. In their stead we find poems dealing with the immediate scene although suitable to any historic time, past, present, or future—the wonder evoked by spring, by the beauty of flowers, by twilight and other natural phenomena, and by the emotion of love. In addition, the poet's language becomes far less extravagant; the rich and vaguely sensuous gives way to the more precise and definite, yet manages to convey impressions that are sensuous and emotionally charged. Word spacing, syntactical distortion, and all the typographical oddities for which Cummings is known are motivated by the same desire to capture, by heightening the impression, the essence of the phenomenon perceived. However, through all this experimentation in the early poetry, his fundamental belief in the importance of sensual perception remained steadfast.

An example of the greater precision of language that Cummings was evolving may be noted in a poem in praise of spring, from *Tulips and Chimneys*. Spring is addressed as a "slattern" who syncopates the world in ragtime ("ragging the world"), who engenders a tremendous nervous energy, discordant and shrill, in all the visible forms of life.

> the grass
>
> rises on the head of the earth
> and all the trees are put on edge

On a first reading the phrase "put on edge" may seem to be nothing more than a cliché supporting the meaning of the preceding line—that of an almost excruciating thrill of response to the potency of spring. However, a little more consideration reveals that Cummings has added dimension to the hackneyed expression, for behind it we recognize all the bursting force of buds and leaves that occurs at the circumference of the tree, at the "edge." Here Cummings has restored vitality to a phrase that had become worn out and meaningless. In context the entire line becomes quite powerful, for we apprehend once again the full significance of the phrase and are startled by its essential correctness in defining growth. The justification of the term is made through the sensory observation of sight; and the impulse of the entire poem is inherent in the line—that of wild and rapid and jarring response. Conceptually the poem indicates that for Cummings spring is affirmation and growth.

The degree to which Cummings stresses the sensual impression as a basis for arriving at meaning or truth about existence varies from the direct statement to the recorded impression of an experience or incident. Midway between these two extremes may be found an occasional poem which indicates Cummings' tenet by contrast; that is, the effect of living by sensory response is compared to that of living by mores, codes, and rules.

Following are a few examples of direct statement, the first from *&* and the others from *XLI Poems:* "let's live suddenly without thinking/ under honest trees, . . ."; "for my friend, feeling is the sacred and agonizing proximity to its desire . . ."; "my mind is/ a big hunk of irrevocable nothing which touch and taste and smell and hearing and sight keep hitting and chipping with sharp fatal tools"; "when my sensational moments are no more/ unjoyously bullied of vilest mind . . ."

One of the best statements of the primacy of sensory perception occurs in a poem from *is 5*. The wit in this poem is striking, for it relates conventional behavior in love to conventional punctuation in prose. And the poem is a comment on Cummings' belief that neither heightened perception nor greater sensory immediacy can be gained through conventional punctuation and syntax which have been dulled by constant use.

> since feeling is first
> who pays any attention
> to the syntax of things
> will never wholly kiss you;
>
> .   .   .   .   .
>
> for life's not a paragraph
>
> And death i think is no parenthesis

The statement of this poem is subtle; however, as a comment by the poet on his own poetic practice it provides the key to an understanding of the spirit and attitude in which the poems were written. Indirectly the poem pays tribute to the necessity of established syntax. However, the poem also states that to realize completely an emotion, a feeling, or an impression, it is necessary to ignore the "syntax" (rules, laws, decorum) "of things" (society, history, tradition). Lovers, in order to appreciate their love fully, establish their own rules; their responses to each other are immediate and spontaneous. They kiss when the desire to kiss is greatest, when they as lovers most want to kiss, and not when the time is proper or the place most fitting according to "the syntax of things." Moreover, as true lovers they will find that life is not a part of something else ("a paragraph"), but an entirety in itself, perhaps *the* entirety; just as certainly they will find that "death" is not a "parenthesis," but rather a spiritual extension of life through love.

Since conventional syntax is often incapable of capturing the complete essence of an impression, a perception, or an emotion, it is necessary to devise a new syntax and a more fitting typography. Throughout his career Cummings followed this practice in the distortion of word, line, and punctuation, thereby achieving a spontaneity that does not allow the reader to observe the poem from a distance, but insists that he involve himself as the poet was involved, that he reconstruct where the poet has constructed. Behind the practice, of course, is the belief in the supremacy of the senses in arriving at the truth about existence.

Cummings also indicates the pre-eminence of feeling by contrasting the effect of seeing natural phenomena as illustrations of some system of classification with the effect of seeing them unhampered by mental categories. The poem

"O sweet spontaneous," from *Tulips and Chimneys,* is an example of such a contrast. Other poems using this same device are "i was sitting in mcsorley's" (in &) and "when life is quite through with" (in *XLI Poems*). One of the more obvious examples is the following poem from *Tulips and Chimneys.*

somebody knew Lincoln somebody Xerxes

this man: a narrow thudding timeshaped face
plus innocuous winking hands, carefully
inhabits number 1 on something street

Spring comes
                  the lean and definite houses

are troubled. A sharp blue day
fills with peacefully leaping air
the minute mind of the world.
The lean and

definite houses are
troubled. in the sunset their chimneys converse
angrily, their
roofs are nervous with the soft furious
light, and while fire-escapes and
roofs and chimneys and while roofs and fire-escapes and
chimneys and while chimneys and fire-escapes
and roofs are talking rapidly all together there happens
Something, and They

cease(and
one by one are turned suddenly and softly
into irresponsible toys.)
                  when this man with

the brittle legs winces
swiftly out of number 1 someThing
street and trickles carefully into the park
sits

Down.   pigeons circle
around and around and around the

irresponsible toys
circle wildly in the slow-ly-in creasing fragility
—. Dogs
bark
children
play
-ing
        Are

in the beautiful nonsense of twilight

and somebody Napoleon

Through the scene of vitality moves a man who is apparently so engrossed in some abstraction or fact that has nothing to do with the immediate present (indicated by the allusions to Lincoln, Xerxes, and Napoleon) that he is completely oblivious to the life around him. This man, a "somebody" who could be anybody because of his absorption in dead things, is a nonentity. By contrast even with the houses which are "lean and definite" in response to "Spring" and which take on human qualities of nervousness against the skyline at twilight, this man merely "winces" and "trickles." His is a routine existence as indicated by his "thudding time-shaped face" and by the fact that he "carefully/ inhabits" a digit room on no specific or particular ("someThing") street. The capital *T* stresses the man's fascination with data, with facts. The word "Down" is capitalized to indicate the direction of the man's vitality. The word "They" (referring to the "fire-escapes and roofs and chimneys") is capitalized to suggest that these objects are more alive and real than the man who denies them because he is unaware of them and particularly of the vitality that twilight seems to infuse in them. The words "slow-ly-in creasing" are so written to suggest the gradual process of fading light (which corresponds with a slower reading tempo). By setting off the word "creasing" there is a pictorial suggestion of the horizontal banderoles that form against the sky at sunset. The explicit contrast comes in that part of the poem which mentions the dogs and the children. By ellipsis, the words "bark" and "play" are present participles, both taking the "-ing" suffix, printed only once. Cummings can pay no higher compliment to a person than to say that he *is*. The present tense of the verb *to be* embodies all the vibrant qualities of response through the senses, of an awareness of life. Hence, the dogs and children "Are." By ellipsis they "Are" alive; and the verb is capitalized to emphasize their alive quality in comparison with the dead conception of "somebody Napoleon" or the man so absorbed with the past that he himself has lost all contact with the actual world which alone can pronounce him a human being.

The majority of Cummings' early poems neither state nor indicate by contrast that sensory perception is the only valid test of reality; rather they proceed on this assumption. As poems they deal with experiences or impressions that in themselves may seem slight. Their intention seems to be merely that of reproducing the emotional sensation of physical love, of response to the natural manifestations of life, of response to vivid childhood memories, or of the felt reaction towards sterility. Behind these poems there resides no implicit body of ideology or philosophic idea. Rather the attempt seems to be that of recording an impression or experience in such a way that the reader is compelled to share it with the poet.

Hence, in the early volumes of Cummings' works, we have love poems that are quite frankly sensual paeans to the physical aspect of love—and nothing more. Numerous poems are addressed to spring and other natural phenomena which stir a human impulse toward pure sensory response. Perhaps the most highly regarded of these eulogies is the poem numbered I under "Chansons Innocentes" in *Tulips and Chimneys*. Some few poems, such as "hist whist" in *Tulips and Chimneys,* are superb re-creations of the enchanted mood of wonder which is a child's in a world full of amazing objects.

Cummings' early poetry also indicates that through reliance on the simple sensory response it is possible to perceive the negative and unproductive experiences of life. Unlike the poems that were to appear later, few of the early poems refer to specific human endeavors or areas of activity in the social scene. Instead, like many of the love poems, merely the emotional reaction to a situation or experience is presented. This intention emerges most clearly in the sonnets Cummings has termed "Realities." Less often can the reader feel assured that the poet's attitude toward his subject matter was either positive or negative in the poems subtitled "Portraits" in the first three volumes of poetry. Because in a number of the early poems value statements of either good or bad have been studiously avoided, and in their stead graphic or sensory detail enlisted, the reader may find himself at a loss to interpret the impression he receives. That an impression has been received is not to be denied, or that the impression of the object or experience described is quite often startlingly vivid; but the problem for many of Cummings' readers (both those who have defended and those who have attacked his practice) is that the impression seems to exist in a void, that there is no indication whether the object or experience described is to be accepted or rejected as a value. The only recourse is to turn to the connotative values of the words employed in the poem; but often this method of evaluation seems inconclusive, for it soon appears that a contrast of connotative values has been established within the poem, which results in an ambiguity difficult to resolve.

Some of the early poems will help to illustrate the foregoing remarks. The purport of the poem in *Tulips and Chimneys* beginning "the Cambridge ladies who live in furnished souls" is clear. More difficult to interpret is the following poem from *&,* listed as a "Portrait."

> being
> twelve
> who hast merely
> gonorrhea
>
>   Oldeyed
> child, to
> ambitious weeness
> of boots

tiny
add
death
what

shall?

Here we have only a few blunt details, a lurking question
mark, and the word "death." If anything, the poem seems
to ask how this child, a symbol of death, comes about, how
she happens to exist in a civilized society. If there is indictment at all, it is not directed toward anything mentioned by
the poem, but toward the reader who has refused to recognize the subject of this poem and what it implies. Death here
is the negation of love and the lack of human feeling that
result in just such children. The poem asks the reader to
respond to a phenomenon of human existence, not merely
to classify it and then conveniently forget it.

Another poem from the same collection, also listed as a
"Portrait," begins:

here is little Effie's head
whose brains are made of gingerbread

On a superficial reading, it seems to present a humorous
eccentricity of the poet's—an apparent lack of respect for
the intelligence or worth of women. However, the satiric
tone is not directed toward Effie as a representative of
women in general but toward Effie's own character as represented by the six crumbs of gingerbread. Effie, who is now
dead, in one sense of the word has always been so, has
never been alive; for the modes of her living were "may,"
"might," "should," "could," "would," and "must." The aux-

iliaries represent doubt, hesitation, lack of security; the imperative quality of "must" represents decorum and regulation. Effie, while alive, never followed one of her own impulses without first examining it in the light of established convention; in short, she has never known or appreciated the significance of what the word *response* means for Cummings. God is indeed puzzled, for the six crumbs left to represent Effie at judgment day are unnatural; nothing of Effie remains to indicate that she ever had a soul. Doomed and damned while alive, her lot unescapably must remain with the "innumerable capering damned." Cummings has said as much in a later poem (from *50 Poems*): "hear/ye!the godless are the dull and the dull are the damned."

These three poems, although possibly varying in the degree of difficulty they present to the reader, nevertheless depend largely for their effect upon an emotional reaction to the images and details presented. With some knowledge of Cummings' basic attitudes toward living (his themes), the poet's intention can be clearly seen. Some of Cummings' poems, however, seem to present an unresolvable ambiguity toward the subject of the poem. What is certainly one of Cummings' most famous anthology pieces, "Buffalo Bill 's" (a "Portrait" in *Tulips and Chimneys*), presents an example of this ambiguity.

Buffalo Bill 's
defunct
       who used to
       ride a watersmooth-silver
               stallion
and break onetwothreefourfive pigeonsjustlikethat
                     Jesus

he was a handsome man
                            and what i want to know is
how do you like your blueeyed boy
Mister Death

This poem has been widely admired, possibly for as many
reasons as there have been admirers. Without a doubt it has
much to offer in technical virtuosity. However, my purpose
here is to note what seems to be a discrepancy in the attitude
the poet has brought to the subject of his poem, a kind of
dual response which seems to result from the contrast of a
childhood memory with an adult perspective. The problem
is to determine whether the picture presented of Buffalo Bill
springs out of admiration or disgust. Does Buffalo Bill represent a vital or a sterile impulse? Is the poet's attitude toward
his subject positive or negative?

An examination of the poem reveals that both interpreta-
tions are possible, that, in fact, the two perspectives have
been telescoped in such a way that neither holds precedence
over the other. The purpose of the poem is not to classify
Buffalo Bill as a hero or a fraud, to favor one of two alternatives, but rather to underscore the ambiguous estimate of
the man that already exists. The poem, in short, is a comment upon the fashion of ostensibly discrediting traditions
that are nevertheless substantially maintained.

Rightly or wrongly this poem has been interpreted as a
satiric comment on the American tradition of abundance
wastefully exploited. About the person of Buffalo Bill clings
the myth of the hunter and Indian fighter supreme. However, historical research tells us that many of the marvelous
exploits of this man were a hoax passed off on a gullible

American public eager for any tangible and living evidence of a glorious and golden era forever gone. He never encountered an Indian in warfare during his life. Moreover, even his hunting has lost its glamour. He was a meat supplier for the crews laying railroad track across the West. He presumably holds the record for the number of buffalo shot in one day, but this has become a dubious honor. The killing of buffalo was indiscriminate slaughter, all the more ignominious because only the tongue was taken from the slain animal; carcasses by the hundreds of thousands were left to rot upon the plains, symbols of the unfeeling and willful destruction and waste which is as much a part of the American tradition as the conception, based on a hoax, of Buffalo Bill as a hero. And so Buffalo Bill as hero is "defunct" because his exploits reflect neither true valor nor honor, and because we do not like to be reminded of what he represents of ourselves as Americans.

But alas, the ideal that Buffalo Bill embodied is also "defunct," invalid along with the myths that surrounded his colorful figure. Unlike the legends that are knowingly tolerated, the ideal has been blotted out under the thumb of fraud. The stories about Buffalo Bill are told and retold, but they are punctuated by a lack of belief. The result is an empty tradition thumped for its own sake—"defunct."

Yet, in the very next breath, so to speak, we have the actual man resuscitated; before our eyes appears the furious and seething picture of Buffalo Bill as the rodeo performer, astride his silver horse in the Wild West Show, the idol of all boys' hearts. The impression conveyed is certainly not depreciatory; moreover, it is completely discordant in tone with all that is implied by the word "defunct." To this point in the poem, then, we have, tightly juxtaposed, the adult perspective with the child's adulation of the hero. In the eyes of the child, Buffalo Bill exists as all that he has ever been purported to be by legend. At this point the underlying ambiguity of the poem has been established.

With the placing of the word "Jesus" not only to the extreme right but also two spaces above what can be construed as a phrase in apposition, "he was a handsome man," this basic ambiguity is intensified and insisted upon. The word "Jesus" not only functions as a forceful expletive, but also by reason of its position in the poem introduces a new subject as a correlative to that of Buffalo Bill. Christ also is a figure embedded in myth and legend, also a type of hero, cherished as a symbol but unheeded in practice and hence for all practical purposes in disrepute. Like Buffalo Bill "he was a handsome man"; and here we note that the phrase serves a dual function. The concluding lines of the poem, which are snide in tone, a satiric snicker implying detached sophistication, represent not the poet's attitude per se but the knowing attitude society has developed toward both of these figures. The subject of this poem, then, is the hero in disrepute for reasons that may be valid but in no way detract from what each has come to represent as an ideal. The fact that Death is addressed as "Mister" indicates the formality and propriety with which a sophisticated society regards not only death, but also Buffalo Bill and Christ as well. Here again we have an example of the real significance of a phenomenon in time (Buffalo Bill or Christ) disguised and lost by accretions of factual knowledge and classification.

The difficulty of this poem is apparent: it consists of determining the attitude of the poet toward what he has written about. My analysis, of course, suggests that Cummings would uphold the position of the child who is aware only of the heroic aspects of the subject. Because of the poem's extreme compression, however, and because of the rapid transition between the two implied opposing attitudes, which in the latter part of the poem practically coalesce into one, this conclusion would be most difficult to derive from a reading of the poem in isolation from what Cummings has said elsewhere. To read the poem as a satiric exposé of American extravagance in the figure of Buffalo Bill is to read it on a less subtle level than here indicated; however, it is this level of reading, I suspect, that accounts for the widespread popularity of the poem. *Time* magazine reported (November 3, 1952) that when Cummings went to Bennington College in Vermont to give a reading of some of his poems, "the entire audience of girls arose as he mounted the platform and chanted in unison one of his poems: Buffalo Bill."

Another difficulty in reading some of Cummings' early poetry is that the incidents and sensuous detail employed in a love poem do not always differ appreciably from those of a poem about debauchery and spiritual sterility. The whole group of sonnets subtitled "Realities" in the 1925 collection, &, serves as an example. To realize the poet's intention it is necessary to pay close attention to the modifying words and abstract nouns. Consider the poem "an amiable putrescence carpenters." It is perhaps more obvious in this poem than in some of the others in this group that what Cummings is attempting to present is the experience not of love but of disgust. But the poem contains the basic ingredients of a number of Cummings' love poems: the sensuous impressions of a woman along with the none too subtle implication of the performance of the sex act. The only difference between the sensuous love poem and the poem of sexual debauchery is one of response: the difference between a sense of joy and an awareness of decay. Because the sense impressions are vivid in both types of poem, a casual reading may result only in perplexity as to what the poet's intention may be in each case. The difficulty may be solved only through an awareness of the emotional or connotative value of the words the poet has used. Hence, in the poem I have cited a definite attitude is transmitted through such words as "putrescence," "purrs," "shuddering burrs/ of light," "terrors" (of the mind), "homelessly," and "lips of death."

This poem and others in the group of "Realities" present examples of the abuse of the senses stemming from a destructive impulse, and are comparable in tone to Shakespeare's sonnet beginning: "Th' expense of spirit in a waste of shame/ is lust in action. . . ." Cummings' purpose, however, is not to comment on the negative aspects of lust, but to portray those aspects in all of their squalor. The appeal is to the senses; the attempt is to gain such a sense of immediacy that a feeling of revulsion or nausea is obtained. The poems that result are not pretty but realistic. The terms of description are often brutal and sickening ("gnashing petals of sex," "chewed stump/ of a mouth," "manure-shaped head," "grim ecstasy," "carcass of a girl"). Presented, then, in these poems are the physical sensations of sordidness, carnality, greed, and the impulse toward self-destruction. As poems they seem to represent a phase in Cummings' development and not a basic trend. They appeared in that period after World War I when futility and despair were prominent in belles lettres. The awareness behind these poems appears most clearly in a line such as the following: "since the world's but/ a piece of eminent fragility." It would be incorrect, I think, to assume that Cummings had espoused an attitude of resignation; rather in these poems he is presenting in harsh terms and images the negative results of the lack of self-concern—a lack of respect for self and the individual status.

From an early poetry of exuberance and sensory detail in which values were seldom pointedly stated, Cummings moved during the mid-twenties to a position from which he more pronouncedly rejects the sham values and superficial by-products of social convention. However, the charge that in his middle and later poetry he became so obsessed with his own integrity as an individual that he could neither accept nor find place for the opinions of others is without warrant in the light of the many poems he has written for the express purpose of giving credit and extending praise to those he admired. Equally unwarranted is the assertion that the characters of his poems are so shallowly depicted as to emerge almost entirely as caricatures, intensely presented in objective detail but lacking in substance of thought or feeling. Numerous poems and prose comments indicate the opposite, among them those lauding Hart Crane, Ezra Pound, Froissart, Ford Madox Ford, Picasso, Sally Rand, Jimmy Savo, Sam (whose "heart was big/ as the world aint square)," his father, and Olaf, "a conscientious object-or," to name those that come most readily to mind.

The last mentioned poem, "i sing of Olaf glad and big," from *W* (*ViVa*), is worth examining, for it depicts a character in terms other than caricature, does not depend upon objective detail alone, and demonstrates that thought and feeling are not alien to the poet's heroes.

Although it is difficult to determine just what a critic may be demanding by the terms "thinking" and "feeling" as attributes of character, it is possible to ascribe to Olaf conscious opinion and certain easily recognized emotions. For example, Olaf upholds his opinion about war not through overt retaliation of insult for insult, not through petty schemes of personal revenge—courses obviously not open to him, since in rejecting war he is rejecting cruelty and sadism—but through a patient acceptance of abuse. However, as evidenced in the two remarks ascribed to him, he does not willingly endure the suffering and torture inflicted upon him. He does not conceive of himself as a martyr dying for some cause; he simply has no use for war. Unlike his persecutors, he will not succumb to playing the role of a caricature; he will not allow himself to be typed as one of those regimented for the express purpose of inflicting misery and perhaps death upon others. Olaf's concept of patriotism and loyalty differs from that of the "nation's blueeyed pride," for it has nothing to do with organized killing. Because he will not conform, because he upholds a belief widely accepted as not practical, he emerges as an individual. The role he plays, though patient, is not passive; he retorts from his position of ignoble humility with the only weapon at his disposal—brutal invective couched in terms his tormentors understand. Because Olaf reveres the dignity of the human being, he has pride. Because he cannot help but react when this dignity is denied or rejected, he is capable of anger. Finally, as Cummings pointedly indicates,

Olaf has that rare caliber of courage which compels him to die not for a cause but because of a cause, not for his country but because of his country.

The individual in Cummings' poetry emerges because of the recognition of two basic precepts: that the codes of behavior and accepted belief of society are stultifying, and that the values residing in nature are not perceived or understood by those who subscribe to the dictates of propriety. The result is that the individual is one set apart not because he wants to be, because he prizes a discipline of some kind for the sake of the discipline, but because his integrity warns him that he must constantly beware of doctrine that is false by the test of the unstereotyped response. A brace of poems from *W* (*ViVa*), published in 1931, illustrates this point.

> myself,walking in Dragon st
> one fine August
> night,i just
> happened to meet
>
> "how do you do" she smiling
> said "thought you
> were earning your living
> or probably dead"
>
> so Jones was murdered by
> a man named Smith and
> we sailed on the
> Leviathan

This poem reveals the individual's awareness of the danger of the conformity that results in "earning your living" or being "dead"—synonymous terms for not being alive.

The poem suggests that we murder the individual within ourselves when we accept the popular code of earning a respectable living, for in so doing we sell ourselves not only to a routine but to the values of material comfort. For Cummings life is a response and not an ordeal, not earning a living but learning to live.

The argument of the poem is that of a man talking to himself. The discussion amounts to an exchange of perspectives between the man and the artist, the man who cannot avoid entanglement in his environment and society, and the artist who must avoid such entanglement in order to know them and approach a definition of their reality. The strife between these two components in the same person is continual; it serves as the balance (which at the same time is the basis) for the individual stance: involvement with society yet detachment from it. The imminent danger lies not in the direction of the artist (eccentricity and seclusion) but in the easier direction of the man and those distractions of society that make for conformity and loss of identity. Hence, the speaker of the poem, an individual, exposes himself to the inherent evils of society by "walking in Dragon st," where he meets himself. That is to say, the artist part of the individual suddenly surprises himself by looking at his immediate surroundings through the eyes of the man. Or to put it another way, the speaker of the poem is pondering the difference between himself as an artist and as a member of society. The opening word of the poem, "myself," acts as both the subject and the object of the verb pattern "happened to meet." The participial phrase "walking in Dragon st/ one fine August/ night" is deliberately squinting, modifying both "myself" and "i." The number of specific allusions suggested by the words "Dragon st" are probably infinite; generally, though, the dragon represents the same danger today that it has always represented: the evil confronting society. Unhappily, today's dragon is found within society itself—the pressures exerted upon the individual to conform and thus lose identity. Like the mythological dragon, today's dragon can kill the individual.

The second stanza of the poem personifies those pressures and temptations that confront the man in the form of a "smiling" woman, an apt as well as a traditional figure. The casual greeting " 'how do you do' " carries more significance than may immediately be apparent: the phrase suggests amazement that this man (who is also an artist and thus an individual) has not succumbed like everyone else to a regular paying job or just died, since there is no real distinction between the two. Or put another way, the man, who recognizes distractions and temptations, asks himself (the artist) how he manages to survive, to remain untouched.

The third stanza is a conclusion, an answer, and a determined avowal. "Jones" and "Smith" are names representing the mythical average citizen, the John Does of all the forms and applications across the nation. They are men who have sacrificed their identity to the idea of a society for the privilege of being members of this society. Murder is forbidden by the laws of this society; the murderer is punished by society. This simple fact relieves the Smiths and Joneses of the responsibility of dealing with murder; however, it also relieves them of the privilege of thinking or feeling for themselves. Society began when men first banded together under laws governing their actions for the purposes of mutual and individual protection. The purpose of this society was to prevent atrocities against individuals. Ironically, the purpose of societies has not been realized: murder, individual and wholesale, is as widespread as ever. More ironic and even tragic is the fact that when the individual dispensed with his rights and privileges to think and feel for himself, he created a monster more horrible than the dragon. That monster is the Leviathan, the state, which enforces rigid patterns and deprives men of their freedom. This monster came into being through the efforts of men to find a method of preventing "Smith" from murdering "Jones." This is one way in which the final stanza may be interpreted. It serves as a conclusion to the entire poem.

The final stanza may also be interpreted as an answer which the artist makes to the man, or the individual to the remarks of the temptress. "How do I do it?" we can imagine the individual replying. How does he maintain his identity? How does he avoid reacting and behaving like everybody else? The answer is that he is too fully aware that the moment he accepts the prevalent codes of behavior and thought he has murdered part of himself, the artist. The fact of "Smith" murdering "Jones" is no more awful than that of the individual committing himself to the dead. The act is identical. Smith in murdering Jones deprived himself of freedom—in fact, instigated the whole concept of society and the state as a forceful means of depriving him of his freedom. Were the individual to accept the dictates of society, he would also be accepting the murder of Jones by Smith as unavoidable and natural. The individual cannot accept the concept of the state or the murder of Jones as natural. Attempting to repress one evil with another evil is senseless, as the individual sees. The evil of the state (the Leviathan) came into being to combat the evil of murder (the Dragon). Man, in attempting to subdue force with force, evil with evil, loses his identity to the force and evil which he has created. This interpretation serves as an answer to the question of what happens to the individual who decides to "earn his living."

The final stanza also exists as an avowal of "myself," the comment of the artist to the man; it is a statement of the threat which surrounds them on all sides, that of succumbing to the temptations of "Dragon st" and the inevitable loss of freedom. In effect, the artist is saying that it would be better to starve, not to earn a living, to be physically dead, than to deprive "myself" of the right to think, feel, respond or to commit myself to the spiritually dead. Only incidentally are "Dragon st" and the "Leviathan" specific appellatives, the first referring to the rue du Dragon in Paris, the second to an ocean liner.

This poem describes the struggle that confronts any person who would be an individual in his society. The result of this struggle is not a deliberate removal; it is not nonconformity for the sake of pose, nor is it an espousal of anarchy. Rather he finds himself alone because of his resistance to codes and values which he recognizes as inapplicable to the truth of existence. The companion to this poem shows the same conflict between the individual and social decorum. Both poems, representative of the middle body of Cum-

mings' poetry, examine the place of the individual in society
and present a defense for his existence.

> but mr can you maybe listen there 's
> me &
> some people
> and others please
> don't
> confuse.Some
>
> people
>
> 's future is toothsome like
> (they got
> pockets full may take a littl
> e nibble now And then
> bite)candy
>
> others
> fly,their;puLLing:bright
> futures
> against the deep sky in
>
> May mine's tou
> ching this crump
> led cap mumble some
> thing to oh no
> body will
> (can you give
> a)listen to
> who may
>
> you
>
> be
> any
> how?

down
to
smoking
found
Butts

Noticeable in this poem is the pathos that attaches itself to the tramp, a figure Cummings is particularly fond of as representative of the individual. Both are outcasts, but for different reasons. The tramp is not respectable, is usually destitute of material goods or the hope of them, and is considered unworthy of sympathy or help of any kind. He does not conform; for example, he does not take a job and earn his own living. He is reduced to smoking castaway cigarette butts.

The individual, though not necessarily destitute of material goods, is disreputable, for he also examines "Butts." These "Butts" are the excuses, the rationalizations, and the generalities by which men live and conform and which, as often as not, are handed down from the past. With this interpretation of "Butts," the pathos applies not to the individual, but to the conformists who are reduced to accepting those social conventions that deprive them of their dignity as human beings. The poem is ironic in that the tramp (who is aware of the present, the now, and lives for immediate needs) is more alive than those who see their futures as "bright" by the accepted standards of those who have already made their futures "toothsome." These people are *not alive;* they are not aware of the necessities of the present.

This poem then, like the one preceding, reveals both the process by which the individual emerges and the necessity that compels him to remove himself from the values most people accept. This poem reveals the individual's awareness of the distinction between himself, "me," "some people/ and others." The deliberately posed question "who may/ you/ be/ any/ how?" presumably addressed to the tramp-individual (and correctly so on a superficial level), is more pungently addressed to "some people/ and others." Only the tramp can legitimately ask this question, for he is aware of himself in relation to what is real—the present. What about these people who live in the past or for the future and are not individuals? Who are they and what is to become of them? Cummings has answered the question in his Introduction to the Modern Library edition of *The Enormous Room:* "I feel they don't become: I feel nothing happens to them; I feel negation becomes of them."

Besides rejecting widespread custom and behavior and thus finding himself alone, the individual also finds himself something of an alien because of a love for things so simple as to appear meaningless; he finds himself isolated for ascribing value to phenomena so natural and commonplace that they appear insignificant from the view of a world of affairs.

> may my heart always be open to little
> birds who are the secrets of living
> whatever they sing is better than to know
> and if men should not hear them men are old

This passage (from one of the "New Poems" in *Collected Poems*) as well as the two poems I have quoted set the prevalent tone of the middle body of poetry—defense of the individual. What is important to realize, however, is that this defense is not based upon mere rejection, but is supported by an opposing set of values, which to the poet appear eminently valid.

With the publication of *50 Poems* in 1940 it became evident that the individual of the earlier poems was becoming aware of himself as one who not only exults in love but also practices that love which is the only real ingredient of life. In a sense the individual becomes in the later poems both the embodiment of and the spokesman for the love that reveals the basic kinship of men. The earlier poems reflect an exuberance about the physical aspect of love. Poems published during the 1930's indicate an awareness of love as the force that perpetuates life and existence beyond death through a kind of transcendental communion with the forces of the universe. But not until the later poems do we find the individual as a disciple of and commentator on love, one who brings an awareness of the force and beauty of love into the lives of others through the simple procedure of being his uninhibited self in action and words. To be sure, these later poems dealing with love are more didactic than the earlier ones; where the earlier poems deal largely with the physical sensations of love and as a result are to a certain degree dramatic, with a recognized speaker or actor involved, the later poems proceed much of the time from an uninvolved voice commenting upon those mystic qualities of love that induce growth, renewal, and harmony. In short, the development has been from poems dealing with the sensations of love to those in praise of a realization of love.

The best known of these later love poems are those that metaphorically figure the wonder and strength of love in the form of a recognizable person, verging on a type. Examples would be his father, anyone of "anyone lived in a pretty how town," Sam of the poem "rain or hail," and the knife-sharpener of "who sharpens every dull." The characters in each of these poems are superb examples of the Cummings hero, the individual who lives and practices love, who is an ambassador of love without consciously striving to be, without the slightest trace of altruism, living his life according to the only valid principle he knows, fidelity to self. However, the majority of the later love poems are not so strikingly dramatized; rather they exist as disembodied statements about love, identifiable with the human situation only as we can hear and accept the voice of the poet. The poem "in/Spring comes(no-/one" from *XAIPE,* published in 1950, is an example.

Although not as explicitly defined, the person in this poem continues the tradition of the Cummings hero beginning with the "little lame balloonman" and extending through the organ grinder, the blind beggar, the tramp, and the knife-sharpener. Here we have "a mender/ of things," and the image that comes to mind is that of the itinerant peddler who repaired pots, pans, and other household utensils. Figuratively this man, an individual, represents spring. Like spring he comes unrecognized, almost imperceptibly. The poem lists comparisons that apply to both the man and spring. Like spring, this individual is an embodiment of growth, renewal, harmony, and love, and he instills these attributes in those with whom he comes in contact. In short, he repairs lives: ". . . remaking what/ other/ -wise we should/ have/ thrown a-/ way . . ." Here then, it seems to me, is the epitome of what Cummings' individual represents: a creative, independent person who not only seems inherently to recognize love, but through his very existence awakes in others a joy and response to that love which is vital to life. (Incidentally, the rather subtle stanzaic line balance in this poem—1,3,2,4,1,5,1,4,2,3,1—indicates one of the methods by which Cummings maintains control over his material.)

The majority of Cummings' later love poems are not so dramatically realized, nor are they so simple. Rather they exist as statements about love that for their authority refer to the poet himself and the logic of his observations. One could choose almost at random among the poems on love in the later volumes for the purpose of illustration—for example the following sonnet from *1 × 1:*

> true lovers in each happening of their hearts
> live longer than all which and every who;
> despite what fear denies,what hope asserts,
> what falsest both disprove by proving true
>
> (all doubts,all certainties,as villains strive
> and heroes through the mere mind's poor pretend
> —grim comics of duration:only love
> immortally occurs beyond the mind)
>
> such a forever is love's any now
> and her each here is such an everywhere,
> even more true would truest lovers grow
> if out of midnight dropped more suns than are
>
> (yes;and if time should ask into his was
> all shall,their eyes would never miss a yes)

This sonnet employs almost entirely abstractions—an ironic thing for a poet who upholds the supremacy of the senses and the validity of only that which can be felt and perceived. If this is a paradox, it is one that Cummings perhaps could not avoid; for if, as he says, "love is a mystery," then love and its significance can best perhaps be defined in poetry through intangibles and abstractions. At any rate, the love poems in Cummings' later volumes depend heavily upon abstract terms for their statement. Most curious, however, as this poem and others reveal, is the fact that very often Cummings, within the mode of abstractions, derides the categorical generalizations that result from abstractions. The effect is very close to parody, ridicule of an intellectual convention of much the same sort as Shakespeare's ridicule of the literary convention in the sonnet "My mistress' eyes. . . ." In either case it seems the poet succeeds indirectly by noting the stultifying aspect of the tradition and yet, by posing his subject within the terms of the tradition, achieves through contrast a startling effect of fresh perception.

Turning to the sonnet, we note that the opening statement is about a quality of love—its endurance. Love endures beyond time; nothing else within the limits of man's mind, because it is circumscribed and finite, so endures. Love, because it is unknown and beyond the limits of man's mind, is infinite. Very broadly, this is the argument of the poem, based upon the two abstractions of love and time. Time, which obliterates all else, is itself obliterated by love. Behind this sonnet is the entire development of Cummings' canon which tells us that the individual, the lover, the poet, is one so continuously aware of man's constant failure and inevitable doom ("mere mind's poor pretend/ —grim comics of duration" and "if out of midnight dropped more suns than are") that he responds to the concept of *nothing,* realizing that all systems of thought eventually dissolve and prove absolutely nothing. And so individuals capable of love reply only to the "happening of their hearts," the feeling of love. Here is the appeal of the senses, which Cummings never foregoes, stated in abstract terminology. To love and be in love is to be in harmony with what exists, the here and the now ("such a forever is love's any now/ and her each here is such an everywhere,"). As the third, fourth, fifth, and sixth lines of this poem indicate, to propound answers to eternal and unknown enigmas is to conclude, and to conclude is death; but for love and growth and hope and dreams there is no conclusion, no ending, but only perpetuity. The individual is aware of this continuous life and growth only through the senses, by responding to the existence of love, for example, not through any philosophic or systematic process of thought, but through the feeling heart.

The more explicit statement of this poem is not very different from the implicit statement of "in/Spring comes(no-/ one." Both poems uphold the supremacy of love as the major contribution of the feeling individual toward the things he perceives, his environment, his society, his universe. The latter poem, ironically, employs intangible definitions to demonstrate the fallibility of categorical generalizations. Hence lovers, who are timeless and immortal, are contrasted to the limited and categorical generalizations of the mind: "which," "who," "fear denies," "hope asserts," "disprove," "proving," "doubts," "certainties," etc. The effect is a kind of parody of abstract thinking through the use of abstract terms. The attitude of the poet seems to be one of saying that if it is abstraction you think you understand, then understand the abstraction of the heart, which can love, in comparison with the formulated abstractions of the mind: the heart is infallible, infinite, and positive, the mind fallible, finite, and negative.

What growth or depth has Cummings' poetry revealed over the years? From my observations I would say that the poet has steadily approached an ideal which can be summarily stated as follows: the purpose of life is the realization of love. Love, however, to be realized, depends upon an individual who applies to himself for the truth as it is perceived and felt.

5. Satire

not for philosophy does this rose give a damn
                                                —*is 5*, 1:33

Cummings is as passionately concerned with those forces in the world that debilitate as with those that nourish. The integrity of the individual and his ability to realize love depend upon his apprehension of vitality through the senses. Forces that stultify the natural, the spontaneous, the vital in life, Cummings sees as antagonists to be exposed, ridiculed, or scorned to oblivion. Who or what specifically are these antagonistic forces? They are people who have lost the ability to feel or respond to the truth of their existence. They are people who do not know themselves as individuals. They are the slogans and formulas that condition human beings to respond like Pavlov's dogs.

Machinemade "civilization" isolates every human being from experience(that is, from himself)by teaching mankind to mistake a mere gadgety interpretation(e.g.the weatherman's prediction)of experience for experience itself(e.g.weather). . . . The "modern man" equals a defenceless literate bombarded with slogans mottoes pictures and whatever else will tend to unmake him;i.e.make him need something unnecessary (*EIMI*)

The product of these destructive forces Cummings has described (in a poem in *50 Poems*) as "a peopleshaped toomany-ness far too" and "a notalive undead too-nearishness." Cummings knows that persons who do not know themselves as unique beings cannot love. Hence he inveighs against human behavior that is void of love (war, collectivism, class hatred, etc.) and those people who give their support to loveless schemes and programs. Sensory perception, self-awareness, and love reciprocate and complement each other for persons who create. Those whose lives are void of love cannot create, Cummings tells us. Empty lives beget only emptiness.

. . . (and Love,what is Love to you?nothing!you create nothing;therefore you cannot Love,and because you cannot Love you create nothing)—(*EIMI*)

Cummings wrote poetry for the purpose of discovering himself; the purpose of his satire was to preserve himself, his identity as an individual. In contrast to what he celebrated (birth, growth, love, joy), there is what he impugned (hypocrisy of any kind, cruelty, unfeeling disregard for human dignity, and death regarded as complete cessation). At its best, Cummings' satire reveals the joy of knowing and discovering ourselves in an amazing if not fantastic world versus the ever-present danger of losing ourselves in a human mass, of succumbing to concocted stimuli presented on a massive scale. On this level his satire is brilliant revelation: trenchant, penetrating, sometimes explosive in its humorous ribaldry. At times, however, the reason for the poet's scorn seems to be lost in a barrage of abuse and name-calling. When this happens two things are apparent: precision of statement is lacking, and the attack seems to be launched from a position in itself conventional and stereotyped. These two failings are, of course, related; when the poet is not himself, he cannot write like himself. Good satire depends upon more than a personal bias: it is based upon the assumption that human dignity is more to be cherished than all or any forms or manners of living.

The basis of Cummings' satire is the unfulfilled ideal of human dignity he cherished. For Cummings human dignity could not exist without love. For this reason he often assumes the role of the iconoclast, jeering at the loveless forces of the world. Enlightened men know they can move toward the perfection of an ideal only through the exchange of opinions, freely given and freely accepted. The satirist contributes to this exchange by presenting harsh, brutal reality in no uncertain terms, trying to make people less than comfortable in their estimates of themselves. While this role is often considered a destructive one, both by the satirist himself and those who are the butt of his satire, in actual practice his basic motive is love and concern for the welfare of himself and hence others. This recognition of motive is one of the great insights a satirist can have, for it suggests a transcendence of individual self into a perfected or perfecting community of men.

Evidence that Cummings was fully aware of this motive

can be found in the dialectic of at least one of the poems, in the statement of another, and in the morality play *Santa Claus;* but nowhere is his recognition more unmistakably presented than in what he has called "A Foreword to Krazy." [1] In this foreword he not only defines the symbolic roles of George Herriman's comic-strip characters—Krazy Kat, Ignatz Mouse and Offisa Pup—but he also explains the position in which the satirist (who by the very nature of his role is an individual) finds himself. Cummings' discussion is cogent for what it reveals about the motive of his own satire.

Krazy, Cummings tells us, represents the ideal of democracy. Offisa Pup and Ignatz Mouse are the hero and villain respectively, "a hero whose heart has gone to his head and a villain whose head has gone to his heart." (This statement coincides with Cummings' belief that society will never reach a millennium through a saving idea or system of thought—something gone to the head—and that such dangerous assumptions can be counteracted and corrected only by the feelings of the heart.) Offisa Pup represents "the will of socalled society" while Ignatz Mouse "forcefully defies society's socalled will by asserting his authentic own." Ignatz Mouse, of course, is the brickbat wielder and as such may be equated with the individual, the satirist, and Cummings himself.

The motive of love as the force behind satire is explained by Cummings through an analysis of Krazy's response to the brick and Ignatz Mouse's reaction to Krazy's response.

---

[1] E. E. Cummings, "A Foreword to Krazy," *Sewanee Review,* LIV (April–June, 1946), 217–221. Included in George J. Firmage, ed., *E. E. Cummings: A Miscellany* (New York: Argophile Press, 1958).

. . . She doesn't, moreover, "love" someone who hurts her. Quite the contrary: she loves someone who gives her unmitigated joy. How? By always trying his limited worst to make her unlove him, and always failing—not that our heroine is insensitive (for a more sensitive heroine never existed) but that our villain's every effort to limit her love with his unlove ends by a transforming of his limitation into her illimitability. If you're going to pity anyone, the last anyone to pity is our loving heroine, Krazy Kat. You might better pity that doggedly idolatrous imbecile, our hero; who policemanfully strives to protect his idol from catastrophic desecration at the paws of our iconoclastic villain—never suspecting that this very desecration becomes, through our transcending heroine, a consecration; and that this consecration reveals the ultimate meaning of existence. But the person to really pity (if really pity you must) is Ignatz. Poor villain! All his malevolence turns to beneficence at contact with Krazy's head. By profaning the temple of altruism, alias law and order, he worships (entirely against his will) at the shrine of love.

Obviously, the motive of love is never apparent, is always submerged in the recognizable motive of replacing ignorance and hypocrisy with hard reality. It is the acceptance of the satiric thrust, the brick on the head, that always amazes Ignatz, the satirist; for he invariably discovers that he is contributing to understanding and love through what is accepted as a token of love—the knock on the head.

Cummings' conviction that the work of the satirist is a labor of love, whether he is fully aware of his motive or not, is again expressed in his summary comment. Indicated as well in this statement is the responsibility of the individual, which he fulfills for his fellow human beings by being true to himself.

. . . Always (no matter what's real) Krazy is no mere reality. She is a living ideal. She is a spiritual force, inhabiting a merely real world—and the realer a merely real world happens to be, the more this living ideal becomes herself. Hence—needless to add—the brick. Only if, and whenever, that kind reality (cruelly wielded by our heroic villain, Ignatz Mouse, in despite of our villainous hero, Offisa Pup) smites Krazy—fairly and squarely—does the joyous symbol of Love Fulfilled appear above our triumphantly unknowledgeable heroine. . . . The meteoric burlesk melodrama of democracy is a struggle between society (Offisa Pup) and the individual (Ignatz Mouse) over an ideal (our heroine)—a struggle from which, again and again and again, emerges one stupendous fact; namely, that the ideal of democracy fulfills herself only if, and whenever, society fails to suppress the individual.

The admission of love as the motive for satire is inherent in the morality play *Santa Claus*. Here, presented dramatically, is the symbol of love, Santa Claus, confronted with the problem of not being able to give away understanding, a corollary of love. However, disguised as Death and construed as Science, Santa Claus finds that he has no trouble selling knowledge as represented by shares in a nonexistent "wheelmine." The result is chaos among the people. At the instigation of a little girl who recognizes him, Santa Claus returns to his original role and by so doing manages to bring joy into the life of one woman.

Love as the basis of satire is inherent in the role of Santa Claus, who functions as both the direct lyric impulse and the satirical corrective for those misguided people who have accepted dubious values. In either case he is concerned with the dispensation of understanding, although in the

role of a salesman he becomes the tool of satire, so gro-
tesque as to make vivid the sterility of the values the crowd
clings to at the expense of love. Although Santa Claus, for
the time that he masquerades as Death and a salesman, may
lose his own understanding of himself, his role in the morality play as the symbol of active love never wavers. This is
as much as to say that the impulse behind Cummings'
lyricism and his satire is one and the same.

In the poetry, love as the impellent of vituperation and
even hate is bluntly identified in the following passage from
a poem in *is 5*. At the same instant the poet notes that this
force is responsible for joy and the feeling that gives rise
to lyricism. Of course, as a paradoxical phenomenon this
fact is widely recognized.

> —what does it all come down to? love? Love
> if you like and i like, for the reason that i
> hate people and lean out of this window is love, love
> and the reason that i laugh and breathe is oh love . . .

Finally, Cummings has written an entire poem (included
in *XLI Poems*) around the simultaneous convictions of
love and hate, residing together, side by side, in the same
breast. The speaker of the poem seems to be saying that he
is drawn by love to people for the very weaknesses and
frailties that make them human, but that he is revolted by
the very blindness that perpetuates these frailties at the expense of the soul and life itself. The poem begins:

> Humanity i love you
> because you would rather black the boots of
> success than enquire whose soul dangles from his
> watch-chain which would be embarrassing for both

but it ends:

> and because you are
> forever making poems in the lap
> of death Humanity
>
> i hate you

Without an awareness of what Cummings considers the motive of satire, a reader is likely to come to the unjustifiable conclusion that the poet is only bitter, that he is something of a cynic, that he is inhabiting the ghost-town of solipsism, or that he is skating along the brink of nihilism. These charges have been made; and they have probably been made out of shock or amazement at the vituperation Cummings unleashes against the forces of negation which he loathes. But there is always the other side of the coin: Cummings never stops expressing his admiration, respect, and love for the vital. As he pointed out, love expresses itself through both affirmation and denial.

For the purposes of discussion, a somewhat tenuous distinction may be made between the general and the specific in Cummings' satire. The general satire does not lampoon a single person or social phenomenon in itself, but instead wittily (and often caustically) ridicules abstract traits peculiar to people in general but alien to the individual: apathy and dullness, insensitivity to beauty, knowledge without understanding, blind adherence to creed and decorum and regulation, dependence upon the mind alone for truth, respectability, conformity, arrogance, provinciality, hypocrisy, and greed. Consider these examples, taken from poems that for the most part are general in their indictment. The first is from *W* (*ViVa*):

> Rain is no respecter of persons
> the snow doesn't give a soft white
> damn Whom it touches

The next two are from *no thanks:*

> . . . p.s. the most successful b.o.fully speaking
> concession at the recent
> world's fair was the paytoilet

> the cult of Same is all the chic;

From "New Poems" in *Collected Poems:*

> down with the human soul
> and anything else uncanned
> for everyone carries canopeners
> in Ever-Ever Land

The next two are from *50 Poems:*

> . . . the godless are the dull and the dull are the damned

> buy me an ounce and i'll sell you a pound.

The next three are from *1 × 1:*

> of all the blessings which to man
> kind progress doth impart
> one stands supreme i mean the an
> imal without a heart.

> . . . Progress is a comfortable disease:

> when man determined to destroy
> himself he picked the was
> of shall and finding only why
> smashed it into because

From *XAIPE:*

> open his head,baby
> & you'll find a heart in it
> (cracked)

If the treatment of negative human traits as subjects in themselves results in general satire, then these same traits embodied in a concrete object or represented in an intangible regarded as tangible result in specific satire. Where the general satire states, the specific satire implies. Compared to the general, the specific satire is oblique and depends for its success upon the recognition that its subject either contains or represents a negative attribute that denies truth, blocks the individual perspective, and corresponds to at least one of the invalid abstractions of the general satire. For example, it is not science as science that Cummings ridicules but rather the popular notion that science is the great benefactor of mankind, the cure-all for every evil, the solution for every social problem that arises. In satirizing science, Cummings is ridiculing the tendency of man in society to impute power and authority to an abstraction. He is belittling a notion, for what science represents as an abstraction does not exist except in the minds of men. Witness the current notion that an ICBM equal in thrust and range to those Russia now possesses will solve the differences between two nations. The circle is vicious: knowledge is combatted with knowledge, fear with fear. Left completely out of the picture are the only essentials, love and understanding, properties of the individual. Even more vicious is the fact that in this rationale, which conceives of the workings of science as the solution to human differences, there is no room for the individual. Hence Cummings' specific satire is aimed at those objects or phenomena to which society imputes disproportionate values. As far as he is concerned, any object or person, cult or belief that has robbed man of what is rightfully his, and hence deprived man of a share of his dignity, is open to satire.

Some of the targets of Cummings' specific satire are communism, fascism (collective schemes of any kind that result in regimentation), chauvinism, pseudo democracy, politics and politicians, salesmen, advertising and advertisers, the near hysterical adulation accorded to celebrities, war, science, religion, the hypocrisy of public ceremonies (including funerals and weddings), philosophy, machines, money, businessmen, the concept of mass production, pseudo-literary entrepreneurs, the British, and such recognizable persons (to name a few) as mr universe, F. D. R., and Warren Gamaliel Harding. A casual reading of the canon of his poetry will turn up instances of most of these subjects. For example, one of Cummings' most powerful indictments of communism and fascism is this nursery rhyme parody from *50 Poems:*

> red-rag and pink-flag
> blackshirt and brown
> strut-mince and stink-brag
> have all come to town
>
> some like it shot
> and some like it hung
> and some like it in the twot
> nine months young

The fetish of chauvinism is ridiculed in the sonnet from *is 5* beginning:

> "next to of course god america i
> love you land of the pilgrims' and so forth oh

Politics and politicians draw a large share of Cummings' disdain. The two epigrams below are typical; the first is from *no thanks,* the second from *1 × 1.*

> IN)
>   all those who got
>   athlete's mouth jumping
>   on&off bandwaggons
>   (MEMORIAM
>
>   a politician is an arse upon
>   which everyone has sat except a man

Perhaps the most direct satire of the salesman occurs in a sonnet in *1 × 1:*

> a salesman is an it that stinks Excuse
>
> Me whether it's president of the you were say
> or a jennelman name misder finger isn't
> important whether it's millions of other punks
> or just a handful absolutely doesn't
> matter and whether it's in lonjewray
>
> or shrouds is immaterial it stinks

Satire of advertising and advertisers, machines, money, businessmen, and the concept of mass production seems to predominate in the volume *is 5*, published in 1926. For the most part these specific subjects are incidental to the larger purpose of ridiculing the superficial values derived from them, upon which Americans pride themselves. "POEM, OR BEAUTY HURTS MR. VINAL," "MEMORA-BILIA," and "the season 'tis, my lovely lambs" are poems that burlesque these subjects. This excerpt is from the first:

> . . . land of Abraham Lincoln and Lydia E. Pinkham,
> land above all of Just Add Hot Water And Serve—
> from every B. V. D.
>
> let freedom ring

The sterility that results from obsession with money and the pursuit of business affairs to the exclusion of life is presented in a poem from *no thanks,* directed at businessmen and captains of industry, beginning:

> exit a kind of unkindness exit
>
> little
> mr Big
> notbusy
> Busi
> ness notman

It is not the celebrity but the way that he is celebrated that Cummings satirizes. Display, ostentation, and obsequious kowtowing Cummings finds disgusting; in the following poem from *is 5* the satire is heightened through contrast with the individual ("i") reaction. The final effect is achieved through the use of a pun, indicating disgust.

?

why are these pipples taking their hets off?
the king & queen
alighting from their limousine
inhabit the Hôtel Meurice(whereas
i live in a garret and eat aspirine)

but who is this pale softish almost round
young man to whom headwaiters bow so?
hush—the author of Women By Night whose latest Seeds
Of Evil sold 69 carloads before
publication the girl who goes wrong you

know(whereas when i lie down i cough too
much). How did the traffic get so jammed?
bedad it is the famous doctor who inserts
monkeyglands in millionaires a cute idea n'est-ce pas?
(whereas, upon the other hand, myself)but let us next demand

wherefore yon mob
an accident? somebody got concus-
sion of the brain?—Not
a bit of it, my dears merely the prime
minister of Siam in native

costume, who
emerging from a pissoir
enters abruptly Notre Dame(whereas
de gustibus non disputandum est
my lady is tired of That sort of thing

War, science, and religion are subjects Cummings has
often treated satirically; passages or entire poems pertaining
to these subjects have been reproduced elsewhere in this
study. Cummings' best known parody of the machine ("she

being Brand") may be found in *is 5*. He suspects philosophy for the simple reason that it too often loses the contact with reality that sensory perception affords—as he makes clear in this stanza of a poem in *1 × 1:*

> multiplied with infinity sans if
> the mightiest meditations of mankind
> cancelled are by one merely opening leaf
> (beyond whose nearness there is no beyond)

Similar to the satire Cummings levels at celebrities and their followings is that which he directs toward occasions or ceremonies that by nature are private but by tradition have become public. Again it is the hypocrisy, the complete isolation from reality that he ridicules. The religious procession and the marriage have both been subjects for his satire, the former in one of his most brilliant travesties, included in *is 5*.

> candles and
>
> Here Comes a glass box
> which the exhumed
> hand of Saint Ignatz miraculously
> inhabits. (people tumble
> down. people crumble to their
> knees. people
> begin crossing people) and
>
> hErE cOmEs a glass box:
> surrounded by priests
> moving in fifty colours
> ,sensuously

(the crowd
howls faintly
blubbering pointing

see
yes)
It
here
comes

A Glass
Box and incense with

and oh sunlight—
the crash of the
colours(of the oh
silently
striding)priests-and-
slowly,al,ways;procession:and

Enters

this
    church.

toward which The
Expectant stutter(upon artificial limbs,
with faces like defunct geraniums)

In the above poem and the poem that follows, what is being ridiculed is not the genuine feeling of piety or worship or love, but the idolatry of the symbols used to represent these feelings. Likewise, in a wedding, the trappings have become more important, receive more attention, and are thought to be more real than the love of a man and a woman. For example, see the poem "this little bride & groom are" in

"New Poems" from *Collected Poems*. The innocent mien with which Cummings satirizes this kind of hypocrisy is superb.

The basis of Cummings' jests at the British is difficult to determine from the two or three instances that appear in his poetry. Possibly nothing more than a jab is intended, an explanation that might also apply to his comments on Jews and snide jabs at Yale. The following is from "New Poems":

> Q:dwo
>> we know of anything which can
>> be as dull as one englishman
> A:to

One of Cummings' most vitriolic condemnations of any person is the poem "F is for foetus(a" (from *XAIPE*), directed at the late President Roosevelt. The poem is primarily abusive, depending for its effect on the force of expletive rather than on any device of precision or witty association. The device by which the poet ends this poem, "honey swoRkey mollypants" is one I have termed phonetic ambiguity: generally, the phonetic spacing of a word or group of words so as to render two distinct applications. Here the transliteration of the French (*honi soit qui mal y pense*) into a kind of English phonetic produces on the one hand an amusing combination of sounds with rather obvious connotations, and on the other an explicit statement.

Not all of Cummings' satire has found its expression in poetry; although not widely known, some of his most interesting satire exists in prose and dramatic form. Much of the play *Him,* for example, is a travesty on forces that rob the individual of his identity. The satiric sketch "Mr. X" lampoons regimentation, mechanization, and gigantic industrialism. X, of course, stands for unknown, a symbol Cummings reinforces with this opening sentence: "Mr. X was one of those inscrutable people who do not exist." Mr. X works in a Wheel Mine (a term Cummings used again in the morality play *Santa Claus*), a structure so large and elaborate that for a worker such as Mr. X there is no way to identify himself. Similarly, the Wheel Mine is so needlessly complicated as to point up clearly the satire of regimentation. And again, the view from Mr. X's front window as described by Cummings is a burlesque of that regimentation which is the result of mass production.

And the Workers' Home being a model Workers' Home, the view from Xs' front window was always different. Sometimes it consisted of Mr. X's underwear and it sometimes consisted of Mrs. X's underwear and it consisted sometimes of the children's underwear (and sometimes of Mr. & Mrs. X's and the children's and sometimes of Mr. and Mrs. X's and sometimes of Mr. X's and the children's and sometimes of the children's and Mrs. X's) but never, never, for any reason, under any circumstances, did it consist of nobody's. When Mr. X arose, of a twilight, he opened his eyes on underwear and when Mr. X retired, of a twilight, he shut his eyes on underwear.[2]

Cummings' contempt for propaganda and patriotic fervor during wartime is revealed in a comment he appended to some of his poems printed in Oscar Williams' anthology, *The War Poets*.

[2] "Mr. X," *Bookman*, LXVI (September 1927), 39–40. Included in George J. Firmage, ed., *E. E. Cummings: A Miscellany* (New York: Argophile Press, 1958).

. . . when you confuse art with propaganda, you confuse an act of God with something which can be turned on and off like the hot water faucet. If "God" means nothing to you (or less than nothing) I'll cheerfully substitute one of your own favorite words, "freedom." You confuse freedom—the only freedom—with absolute tyranny. Let me, incidentally, opine that absolute tyranny is what most of you are really after; that your socalled ideal isn't America at all and never was America at all: that you'll never be satisfied until what Father Abraham called "a new nation, conceived in liberty" becomes just another sub-human superstate (like the "great freedom-loving democracy" of Comrade Stalin) where an artist—or any other human being —either does as he's told or turns into fertilizer.

In 1930 Cummings published a collection of eight loosely styled satiric fables. The book itself has no title and the edition was limited to 491 copies. Much of the writing in this book is nonsense, impressionistic, without tangible reference or coherent development, depending for its humor upon obvious absurdities and impossibilities. However, many of the sketches are funny, the humor deriving from the associations of a great number of details huddled together in a particular way. It is from these details that the satire takes its form; for revered objects such as science, business, money, government, politicians, etc., are inextricably bound up with the most exaggerated and inconsistent details imaginable. Two excerpts indicate the general tone of these sketches.

A hookandladder, driven by Abraham Abrahams at a speed of $a + b^{a+b}$ miles an hour, passed over the magnate longitudinally as he crossed Dollar Row and left a rapidly expiring corpse automatically haranguing an imaginary board of directors; and whose last words—spoken into the (oddly enough) unbroken mouthpiece of the instrument only to be overheard by Archibald Hammond, a swillman—were:"Let us then if you please."

A patented fishnet full of stuffed minnows appeared, closely followed by a royal Bengal conundrum wearing eleven brown derbies and preceded by small-pox.

What is probably Cummings' most intriguing and effective satirical writing outside the poetry is a short play entitled *Anthropos: The Future of Art.* The effect of this play—and it is powerful—depends upon a stark depiction of the two extremes of man's behavior, a contrast between the best that man can achieve, the status of a creative individual, and the worst to which he can deteriorate, the ignoble existence of a completely submissive automaton. This contrast is apparent in the characters of the play: an artist, and a mob of "infrahuman creatures." This contrast is further indicated through the symbols white and black, the white representing light which the artist seeks, the black representing the darkness of oblivion into which the "infrahuman creatures" are sinking.

The motif of light and dark is carried out in the elaborate printing and binding of the play. The front cover is white except for black strips on the vertical edges and the title, which is printed on the white of the cover in bold black ink. The spine is black, with ANTHROPOS imprinted on it in black and white. The back cover is also black. The first three pages are white—the third carrying a reproduction of the title as it appears on the cover. A leaf, black on both sides, follows the title page, and throughout the book these black leaves separate the white leaves on which the text is printed. The design is impressive. Cummings told me that the format and the color arrangement were "entirely due to S. A. Jacobs."

The fifth white page (which bears no number; none of the pages is numbered) presents the setting in the following words printed on the lower three-fourths of the page:

SCENE: one-half of the dim interior of a hemispherical cave. In the foreground—to the audience's left, three uncouth infrahuman creatures smothered in filthy skins squat, warming their gnarled paws at what was once a fire— to the audience's right, a naked man (his back toward the trio) is cautiously, with a few crude painting tools, outlining some monster on the up-curving wall before him. In the central background hangs a curtain of skins: somewhere behind this curtain, a sequence of rattling gushing hissing rumbling clanking noises repeats itself without interruption.

The action of the play is simple. The three infrahuman creatures (who are called *G, O,* and *D* respectively) are debating among themselves the choice of a slogan to pacify an angry mob of dwarf infrahuman creatures over whom they have control. They debate their problem while sitting around the dead embers of a fire. Unnoticed by them an artist—a man who is completely naked because he does not conform to convention; in fact, he cannot conform if he is to create—is industriously applying himself to the painting of some large monstrous-looking thing on the wall before him. The trio of infrahuman creatures finally and spontaneously hit upon the slogan of "Evolution." After agreeing upon their slogan, they whistle for "a muttering snarling grunting squeaking jabbering mob of hide-smothered infrahuman dwarfs," which "angrily seethes down the center aisle toward the footlights." At the command of "At-/ Ten-/ TION!" from the three infrahuman creatures, the "mob freezes into a silent mass whose units punctually and simultaneously salute—the salute is languidly returned by the trio." To this mob it is announced that "the war will soon be over!" and that "Evolution is our ally!" The mob responds with three cheers and marches out in good order. The three infrahuman creatures then congratulate themselves on their success, but almost immediately catch sight of the naked man who has been silently painting during the preceding action. At this point, however, the artist has reached an impasse; he has reproduced the object of his painting to his fullest human ability. Beyond this there is only the object itself. For this reason he wishes to get outside of the cave and into the sunlight to take another look at what he calls a mammoth.

Upon seeing the artist, the three infrahuman creatures shriek in startled disbelief and horror. They call the man a "thing" because they do not recognize him. They refer to him as "it." ("Where does it think it's going?") The man replies that he needs another look at the mammoth. The three infrahuman creatures cannot believe that the artist is sane, that he thinks mammoths still exist. The dialogue which follows is interesting for what it reveals of the deception that engulfs the minds of men who accept slogans instead of reality, traditional beliefs instead of truth.

Man
>   (arms akimbo, frowns):
>   What are you freaks talking about?

First Infrahuman Creature
>   (ardently):
>   Civilization!

Second Infrahuman Creature
>   (fervently):
>   Emancipation!

Third Infrahuman Creature
>   (enthusiastically):
>   Progress!

Man
>   (grins):
>   Don't try to kid me!

First Infrahuman Creature
>   (earnestly):
>   No, reely!

Second Infrahuman Creature
>   (pompously):
>   It's the Ford's truth!

Third Infrahuman Creature
>   (solemnly):
>   So help me Lenin!

At this point the man-artist steps to the skin curtain "and yanks it aside—revealing a jagged cave-mouth and, beyond, a sunlit excavation wherein a solitary rattling gushing hissing rumbling clanking steamshovel is rotating and plunging and rearing and wheeling and spewing." The trio of infra-human creatures are terrified at this apparition; they also recoil from the "instreaming sunlight." They are terrified because for the moment they recognize the truth—and this truth is directly opposite to what they thought was the truth, what they have been taught to believe. For a moment they see the steamshovel not as a product of so-called evolution and progress, but as the artist sees it—a monstrous mammoth, a symbol of mass society. (Note that the adjectives describing the mob of dwarfs and the steamshovel indicate a mechanical, noisy existence void of self-discipline.) The artist, however, instead of being terrified, is only filled with wonder and curiosity. He creeps through the cave-mouth and toward the steamshovel for the purpose of investigation. Significantly, he is creeping toward the sunlight. His response toward this phenomenon is natural; he is curious. He sees this mechanical mammoth as a monstrous thing; but the so-called civilized infrahuman creatures can feel secure only in the shroud of their beliefs. And so they pull the curtain of skin, cut off the sunlight, and once again feel safe in the black night of traditional concept: the steamshovel is only a steamshovel.

This play is a devastating satire of authority without understanding. The contrast in the pages between black and white symbolizes the antithesis between reality and unreality, truth and what is thought to be truth: specifically, the distance between the accepted beliefs peculiar to the mass, stereotyped mind (the blackness of unoriginality), and the sunlight of inspiration and curiosity. The future of art is evidently going to remain with the individual who responds to sunlight. In dramatic terms the play presents an instance of the conflict between unthinking and unfeeling mass-men and the individual who is an artist, who responds to his environment without consulting accepted, prescribed, or traditional belief.

The very speech of the infrahuman creatures is an indication of their loss of identity to widespread custom and behavior in thought and action. They speak in a low mixture of slang and colloquialism.

> First Infrahuman Creature:
> Zowie!

> Second Infrahuman Creature:
> Shoot, G!

> Third Infrahuman Creature:
> Spit it out, G, old man!

> Second Infrahuman Creature:
> Come clean!

> Third Infrahuman Creature:
> Make it snappy!

> Second Infrahuman Creature:
> Let's go!

> First Infrahuman Creature:
> "Nothing succeeds like success."

> Second Infrahuman Creature:
> AWFUL

> Third Infrahuman Creature:
> I should say *not*.

It is interesting to note that, after the slogan "Evolution" is decided upon, the first letter of each of the three comments made by the three infrahuman creatures in congratulating themselves again corresponds to their own names and spells out the word *GOD*.

> First Infrahuman Creature:
> Gee—that's SWELL!

> Second Infrahuman Creature:
> O-BOY!

> Third Infrahuman Creature:
> De - CIDEDLY!

The word "GOD" in the play is used generically, having to do only with the distortion of religious belief into rigid practice and nothing to do with Christianity per se. As a term, "GOD" is ironically equated with "Evolution." "GOD" represents authority that demands an all-embracing, universal, and unquestioning obedience to a presumably infallible concept conveniently expressed in the form of a slogan. The slogan is Evolution. Since the concept of evolution derived from science, the term "GOD" can best be applied to the godhead of our century: Science. It is no accident that the characters in this play are consistently alluded to as "Infra" —to suggest that they are a product of a science of some kind, as indeed they are: the science of mass control through the imposition of mechanical and ritualistic obedience to an idea. Hence the term "GOD." When the artist refers to the steamshovel as a mammoth, the symbology of the play is complete. The steamshovel, a monstrous creation of science, is without sensibility. Imputing authority to an idea and then worshiping it blindly produces the same consequence: insensibility. Cummings would say that this is what has happened to men today. The result of blindly obeying an abstract idea such as the beneficence of science ("Evolution is our ally!") is twofold: man is degraded to an automaton, and the slogans or symbols representing the idea become more real than life itself.

Light, on the other hand, is a symbol of awakened sensibility. It is the light pouring in through the backdrop of skins that brings to the audience an awareness of the steamshovel as a mammoth. In summary, then, it can be said that this play upholds the core of Cummings' artistic tenets: the integrity of the individual. Beyond this the play shows the very real threat confronting men when they refer to something outside of their individual perceptions for the discovery of truth.

It is best to consider Cummings' lyricism and satire together, for both spring from the same motive. The satire complements the lyricism; the lyricism remedies the satire. The effect of attempting to consider them separately is only to realize more clearly their interrelationship. Lloyd Frankenberg has cogently observed that Cummings himself has made the best statement about the essential unity of his lyrics and satire in the opening line of one of his love poems in *1 × 1:*

one's not half two. It's two are halves of one:

6. Techniques and Forms

who pays any attention
to the syntax of things

—*is 5*, 4:7

The danger of unquestioning obedience to the syntax of things is sterility. Cummings loved vitality. ". . . I am abnormally fond of that precision which creates movement," he wrote in the Foreword to *is 5*. It is a comment on his own practice as a poet.

Cummings' name is associated with unconventional punctuation and capitalization, word displacements, and unusual arrangements of stanzas, lines, words, and even individual letters to produce visual typographical forms. His poems range in prosodic shape from the terse, cryptic ideogram (or pictogram), which in appearance may resemble a column of Chinese script, to conventional stanzaic forms with regular line lengths, meter, and rhyme. Most of his poems fall between these two extremes; nevertheless, an unwary reader may mistake a Cummings sonnet for a poem in free verse. In this chapter, with the help of some of his poems,

I hope to show how thoroughly conscious Cummings was of the syntax of things in relation to poetry.

The ideogram is probably Cummings' most difficult form. These most terse of poems combine visual and auditory elements, and must be viewed in much the same way as an intaglio. Sounds are suggested, but they may be onomatopoeic rather than linguistic—that is, heard, associated with a visual image, but not pronounced. Consider the poem "!blac" in *50 Poems*.

!blac
k
agains
t

(whi)

te sky
?t
rees whic
h fr

om droppe

d

,
le
af

a::;go

e
s wh
IrlI
n

.g

The only critical comment on this poem that I know of suggests that the typographical arrangement has "added the entire enormous machinery of a thunderstorm." [1] A statement the poet made in a letter seems more relevant: "for me, this poem means just what it says . . . and the ! which begins the poem is what might be called an emphatic (= very)." [2]

At first glance the reader might think that this poem is a product of caprice. Why write a poem vertically? Why toss punctuation marks around without any apparent regard for their logical or grammatical use? Why divide words between syllables?

After looking at the poem for a while you may begin to see some of its felicities—formality, for example, in the stanzaic pattern of alternating four and one lines. Though the way the words are written may seem to make no sense, sound them to yourself and discover the interesting patterns of sibilant and spirant consonants and internal vowel rhymes. (Specifically the *c*'s, *k*, *t*'s, *te*, a *d*, and *af* combined with the voiceless *s* rhymes in "agains" and "rees" and the vowel rhymes of "(whi)" and "sky" and of "te" with "rees" and "le.") The poet meant these consonants and rhymes to be heard, else he would not have printed them separately. Their sounds were meant as tonal metaphors.

Here is the poem conventionally written out with some of the punctuation deleted: "!black against white sky? trees which from dropped leaf goes whirling" It says next to nothing thus written and, recited aloud to one hundred

---

[1] Robert M. Adams, "grasshopper's waltz: the poetry of e. e. cummings," *Cronos,* I (Fall, 1947), 2.

[2] Letter from Cummings to the author, February 23, 1959.

people, would undoubtedly draw one hundred blank stares. But Cummings has so positioned the words that the falling of the leaf takes on poignancy, and the greatest effect possible in movement, timing, accent, contrast, sound, and ambiguity is achieved. The poem requires to be absorbed rather than simply read.

The exclamation point with which the poem begins indicates that something anterior to the poem has already happened. The poem attempts objectively to describe certain impressions which are the result of—"!"

The first impression is visual—"black against (whi)te"—followed by a feeling of wonder and bemusement as indicated by the phonetic suggestion of why "(whi)" and the question mark. The next impression is that of the sky, then the trees with the realization that from them dropped . . . At this point a comma intrudes itself, and this comma is important for it indicates a pause (its traditional use) and the beginning of a new awareness which is imposing itself and merging with the previous impressions—the awareness of a falling leaf.

Bypassing for the moment the appearance of the words on the page (the intrasyllabic division and the sounds thus produced) and considering their dictionary meanings we recognize that "blac/ k/ agains/ t/ (whi)/ te" applies descriptively not only to the general appearance of limbs and branches against the sky but to the leaf which is in the process of falling. Looking up, the leaf against the white sky looks dark, perhaps even black. Compressed into this descriptive observation—almost simultaneous with it, in fact—elicited by the contrasted symbolic values of black versus white (a second level on which these words operate), we have the beginnings of a conceptual awareness, indicated by the phonetic interrogative "(whi)" and the strategically placed question mark.

It is on the level of perceptive insight and significant awareness that the poem is ultimately addressing the reader. The symbolic accretions which have become associated with the words *black* and *white* are numerous and profound, and any attempt to assign one specific value to the exclusion of others is presumptuous. However, in the light of Cummings' themes it is probably not amiss to realize that inherent in these words are suggestions of the cyclic motions of life and death. On one level this is precisely what this poem is describing: reintegration through death. The falling leaf is a symbol of dying. However, the very process of dying suggests the vibrancy of life, the natural prelude to reintegration with the cyclic motions. This particular vitality of the falling leaf is conveyed through the typography.

Hence we hear the descent of the leaf in the spirant consonants, the rhymes; we almost feel the little breaths of wind in the slight sibilant whisperings. The printing of the word *leaf* ("le/ af") suggests the nautical terms *lee* and *aft,* terms used in reference to the direction of the wind. With the placing of the letter "a" in the line "a:;go" we have a syntactical inversion which allows the letter to function as the article of "le/ af" as well as the article of the time intervals represented by the colon and semicolon. These marks of punctuation operate symbolically in much the same fashion as they operate literally—to indicate pause, sequence, integration. The leaf dropped "a:;go" which is as much as to say a moment or two ago, two impressions ago. While the observer has been noticing the *black against white* (or *white sky*) and the branches of the *trees,* the leaf has been dropping. The colon and semicolon then represent pauses, just as in traditional syntax.

The last three stanzas of the poem, including the words "goes whirling," are spaced and broken to correlate the tempo of the reading with the progress of the leaf downwards through the air. The *i*'s in the word "whirling" are vowel glides and are capitalized to give visual balance to the line and possibly to suggest the glide of the leaf earthward. Finally, the period preceding the letter "g" indicates that although the episode is complete, a larger process of which it is a part is not; that the poem itself is a fragment, part of a continuum; specifically, that although the leaf has come to a conclusion, the cycle of death, renewal, birth, and growth of which the leaf is a part has not. Apart from their individual functions, these technical devices combined produce the over-all appearance of the poem in which we see the actual descent of the leaf on the very page, the words choreographed to suggest the shallow dips, the downward movement with little essays and wind flutterings away from the direct drop.

Cummings published nothing like "!blac" during the Twenties, in his first four volumes of poems. Throughout his career he wrote poems, of course, which can be effectively recited, but it was not until the publication of *W* (*ViVa*) in 1931 that he began publishing poems that could not be read aloud—poems, that is, with elliptical ambiguities, tonal metaphors, and coalesced impressions which the human voice alone cannot convey to an audience. These poems are not numerous at any period, but they are present up through *95 Poems* in 1958. Some of them would be partially intelligible if they were read aloud, and the majority of them are not as abbreviated as "!blac." But all of them use devices that are part of Cummings' unique contribution to the language of poetry. In my opinion a close study of the manner in which Cummings employs these devices is well worth the effort for the purpose of appreciating the corpus of his work.

The ideogram compresses perception, feeling, and realization until they are no longer distinguishable, until, as Keats observed, beauty is truth and truth is beauty. Cummings responded to the beauty of twilight, a first star, the new moon. His purpose in striving for compression in these poems was to realize more fully the truth about love and being alive that he felt resided in something as simple as seeing a flake of snow—or a whole snowstorm. He has written numerous poems on these subjects. But the progress he made in realizing their significance can best be seen by comparing an early poem with a later one—for instance, "in the rain-" from *XLI Poems* with "a-/float on some" from the volume *1 × 1*. They are very much alike in subject matter and in the tone of voice. However, they show a great difference in technical accomplishment, and they illustrate the poet's development, a matter which has concerned many critics.

> in the rain-
> darkness,   the sunset
> being sheathed i sit and
> think of you

the holy
city which is your face
your little cheeks the streets
of smiles

your eyes half-
thrush
half-angel and your drowsy
lips where float flowers of kiss

and
there is the sweet shy pirouette
your hair
and then

your dancesong
soul.   rarely-beloved
a single star is
uttered, and i

think
          of you

In this apostrophe the irregular line lengths, the final
staggered line, the word spacing, and the compounding of
words are devices meant to control the tempo and rhythm
of reading. The images are those Cummings loves—rain,
sunset, flowers, a star—but they seem artfully rather than
artlessly posed. They establish a mood of nostalgia, and
they relate to the physical beauty of the beloved. However,
Cummings wants to say something about the "soul" of his
lady through these images. For this reason he describes her
face as "holy," her eyes as "half-angel." But the integration
of physical beauty and spiritual harmony is not too con-

vincing. There is a progression in the imagery, which leads from awareness of the physical to awareness of the spiritual —the soul. And this progression suggests a comparison: that the feeling evoked by the physical beauty of the beloved in no way differs from the reverent feeling evoked by sunset or the first appearance of a star at twilight. But this comparison is only suggested, not emphasized.

Twenty years later appeared the following poem, identical in its setting of twilight, the address to the beloved, the luminous appearance of, this time, the moon.

a-

float on some
?
i call twilight you

'll see

an in
-ch
of an if

&

who
is
the

)

more
dream than become
more

am than imagine

This poem (an impression), due to its economy of statement and image, makes demands upon a reader that the earlier poem does not. Conflict between the appearance of a new moon at twilight and human apathy gives tension to this poem that the earlier one lacks. Cummings favors the moon, deplores indifference to such vital splendor. But by this time he had found out that the simple reference to those things in life which awe him is not enough: they had to be vitalized on the page. Hence the reader must discover the moon for himself, must realize that this poem and the moon are nearly synonymous. The poem describes the appearance and effect of the moon without once using the word.

The moon as a symbol of growth and change is, of course, particularly apt. Its hovering appearance in the sky when all objects seem to take on an extra dimension is described by the word "float." The moon is both *afloat* and *a float*. Cummings has positioned the word to get its effect as both an adjective and a noun. What is it that sustains the moon, gives it that perfection of poise so complete that it fixes itself in the mind's eye? The poet doesn't know, can only wonder: hence the question mark. The magic of twilight and "you" as an image of love are all part of what invests the moon with awe. There is no transition here. The moon, response to twilight, awareness of the beloved are inseparable. The symmetrical perfection of the moon as it appears in the crystalline twilight and the sense of harmony produced by love are part of the same mystery, which is life. This most meaningful association of perception-response-awareness Cummings wants to convey through his poem.

A comma after the word "twilight" would, of course, render the line capable of being read only one way. As it is, without punctuation, the line is elliptical, enforcing the ambiguity of the word "you." The complete line—"i call twilight you"—functions as both an estimate of love and the address to the beloved, a compliment in the form of a metaphor. The alternate reading is that of "you" as the subject of the verb contraction " 'll see." With this alternate reading the first three words of the line ("i call twilight") revert to what was probably the reader's first impulse, an adjective clause modifying (as illogical as this seems) a nonexistent noun, the unknown represented by the question mark. However, this structure also has its purpose: it comments on the effect of twilight upon visual objects, an unknown quality that lends a depth of perception not apparent at other times. Twilight itself is a mystery. From this point on the poem develops and enforces the implications of the relationship established between the feeling of love and the uninhibited response to the emerging moon at twilight.

The moon, then, is not just an object in the sky, but is as vibrant as love and life itself. For this reason it is personified by the relative "who" and pictorially represented by the single mark of parenthesis. Moreover, the word "who" as it is positioned briefly inherits its function as an interrogative, thereby reinforcing the feeling of wonder and awe suggested by the question mark above. The realization of the moon as an emblem of life and reality, itself alive, is further enforced by reference to the words "dream" and "imagine." These are abstract words representing typically human capabilities. But the poet tells us that the moon is even *more* alive. The moon *is* the dream, not something nebulous and distant, but the personification of what man dreams, the realization of love that man imagines exists. The moon is that harmonious perfection man only dimly perceives— but alive, immediate, in the absolute present. Look at the moon, the poem is saying, and see alive ("more am") the abstract perfections man yearns for in dreams and imaginings. This is the power of Cummings' technique—through the use of abstractions representing values supposedly antithetical to the phenomenal world, to capture and indicate these values as they nevertheless do exist in the present. In effect Cummings is saying that the moon is what you have always known it to be, and not what you have thought it to be, as lifeless as the abstractions for which you yearn. Recognize the beauty and perfection of the present moment and you will realize the harmony and love of the life that actually does exist.

The superficial impressions the appearance of the poem registers on the mind are further supports for the argument of the poem. With Cummings it is the usual rule to find technique and theme interdependent. This fact explains the alternating one-and-three-line stanzas, the positioning of the word "more" in the penultimate stanza (presenting to the eye a sense of balance, to the ear a sense of refrain), and the slant rhymed patterns of consonance in such lines as "an in," "of an if," and "am than imagine." Consonance is also in evidence in the line "dream than become." Because of their brevity these lines also offer visual patterns of balance. Taken together these devices act as provocative support for the significance of the words. The poem itself is an example of that compression peculiar to Cummings which is capable of forcing words to divulge more than we thought they contained, of awakening perceptions beyond language. The poem illustrates that precision which Cummings had been perfecting over the years for the purpose of enforcing the truth of his vision.

Cummings' concern for "the syntax of things"—poetic techniques—found expression in a variety of shapes and forms. The shape of the poem "brIght" in the volume *no thanks* is figuratively meant to suggest a ray of light streaming from its source—a star. Note the way the poem spreads out, the increasing number of lines in each successive stanza. The poem reveals purpose in the unconventional use of punctuation and capital letters. It is also an example of coalesced impressions through parenthetical comment.

> brIght
>
> bRight s??? big
> (soft)
>
> soft near calm
> (Bright)
> calm st?? holy
>
> (soft briGht deep)
> yeS near sta? calm star big yEs
> alone
> (wHo
>
> Yes
> near deep whO big alone soft near
> deep calm deep
> ????Ht ?????T
> Who(holy alone)holy(alone holy)alone

This poem is a kind of abstract metaphor: the denotative meanings of the words act as the specific subject and the emerging visual impression as the metaphoric or connotative element of the comparison. Within the poem the literal and the figurative elements complement each other. To see how Cummings manages this feat is a unique reading experience.

There are two readily understandable explanations for the use of capitals, and both of them apply to what Cummings has called "that precision which creates movement." Any particular star that one may be watching seems to become brighter as twilight deepens through dusk to complete darkness. This is one of the phenomena Cummings is trying to suggest through the use of the capitals; the other is the fact that a star when closely watched seems to emanate light from different points, to "twinkle" as in the nursery rhyme. Thus the word *bright* is written six times in interrupted succession as follows: "brIght," "bRight," "(Bright)," "briGht," "????Ht," and "?????T." All six letters of the word receive at some place in the poem the emphasis of a capital to indicate points of light and the gradual process by which a star emerges.

Two other words in the poem receive this same distinction: *yes* and *who*. Both words appear three times in different formats. The word *yes* is written "yeS," "yEs," and "Yes." The word *who* appears as "(wHo," "whO," and "Who." The application of the capitals in these words corresponds to their use in the word *bright* with this difference: whereas the capitals in the word *bright* enforce a gradually emerging visual impression, the capitals in the words *yes* and *who* are related to the gradually emerging mental awareness of the significance of the visual impression. As the star emerges, its appearance becomes more distinct and positive—*yes*. Yes, the observer is saying, it is a star, and yes, it's alive and real and sparkling. The word *who* supports this contention just as strongly by applying the personal element, usually reserved for animate beings, to the supposedly inanimate star. What we have here, then, is the use of capitals to suggest two correlated movements from the dim and obscure to the sharp and poignantly realized—visual and conceptual awareness.

Easily recognized is the fact that the question marks in the poem stand for the missing letters in the word *star* and in the penultimate line the word *bright*. Again a progression is indicated through this device. The star as it emerges loses one question mark after another until the word appears complete, as does the object it represents: a star. But these question marks do more than just this; they also suggest the wonder and awe one feels before this spectacle which represents growth. In the penultimate line they effect the transition (also mysterious) that has been gradually taking place throughout the entire poem: the transition from what started out as a purely visual awareness to a conceptual and spiritual awareness. The remaining words in this poem also demonstrate this transition, ranging from the early physical descriptive ("big," "soft") to the concluding conceptual and spiritual descriptive ("holy" and "alone"). The progression indicated by the question marks goes something like this: what was definitely "bright" at the beginning of the poem emerges into a star; with the awareness of the star comes a realization that more is represented here than just the physical appearance—hence the question marks to fill out the word *bright* in the penultimate line. What is this something more? It is unknown, mysterious, incapable of explicit definition. At best we can approach the feeling evoked through the words "holy" and "alone."

The parentheses in the poem show a progression in the contemplation of the effect of the star. As the poem proceeds, the parentheses include more words, indicating the growing awareness beyond the purely visual. The parentheses in the final line indicate that what the star appears to be is just exactly what it is, that the word "bright" leads inevitably to the words "holy" and "alone," that finally the visual appearance that may be described as "holy" and "alone" (not enclosed in parentheses) cannot be differentiated from the conceptual and spiritual awareness of the star "(holy alone)" enclosed in parentheses. In short, the poem is saying that the experience of seeing a star is the meaning of life, the mystery of existence, representing birth and growth.

As I have noted, Cummings wrote poems that even Mrs. Grundy would recognize as such. Established stanzaic patterns, strict metrical lines, and rhyme have always been part of his technical repertoire, and poems with these characteristics can be found in every volume of poetry he published. They show a precision, particularly in his later volumes, as meticulous as that found in the ideogram. In addition, traditional forms seemed to allow him more freedom: he indulged in wit, humor, narrative, satire as well as fleeting impressions and brief incidents. The ideogram is a moment of coalesced awarenesses. The poem written in traditional prosody may

be, for Cummings, a philosophical reflection, a complete
episode, a character sketch, or a narrative summary of an
entire life. He put established forms to more uses than he
did the very terse poem of impression. The broader confines
allowed him to investigate more than one perspective, as in
the following poem from the volume *1 × 1*.

it's over a(see just
over this)wall
the apples are(yes
they're gravensteins)all
as red as to lose
and as round as to find.

Each why of a leaf says
(floating each how)
you're which as to die
(each green of a new)
you're who as to grow
but you're he as to do

what must(whispers)be must
be(the wise fool)
if living's to give
so breathing's to steal—
five wishes are five
and one hand is a mind

then over our thief goes
(you go and i)
has pulled(for he's we)
such fruit from what bough
that someone called they
made him pay with his now.

But over a(see just
over this)wall
the red and the round
(they're gravensteins)fall
with kind of a blind
big sound on the ground

The metrics in this poem are flawless except for the last line of the last stanza. Because the metrics are flawless, the poem is disciplined as well by syllabic count. The syllabic pattern for each of the stanzas is as follows: 6,4,5,5,5,6. The last line of the poem is the only deviation; here a five-syllable line is substituted for the six. No metrical foot predominates in this poem; rather there is a perfect alternating pattern of iambic and anapestic feet; each stanza begins with an iamb, follows with an anapest, and then alternates these two feet in perfect sequence throughout the first five lines of each stanza; the final line of each stanza consists of two anapests, the penultimate anapest occurring where the pattern would have indicated an iamb. The only exception is again the last line of the poem; here the alternating pattern of iambic and anapestic feet is completed; the last line consists of an iamb and an anapest instead of two anapests. The scansion pattern is as follows:

SYLLABLES	METRICS
6	x/xx/x
4	/xx/
5	x/xx/
5	x/xx/
5	x/xx/
6	xx/xx/

The last line of the poem, however, offers this variation from the last line of the other four stanzas.

SYLLABLES	METRICS
5	x/xx/

The scansion pattern above allows for subsequent observations: that although the syllabic count varies among the lines, the stresses do not; each line is dimeter. Moreover, the first line in each stanza is the only line which has a feminine ending; as a result the second line in each stanza is the only one that begins with a stressed syllable. The effect this has upon the metrics is that of carrying the second iamb over from the first line to the second line. Since three of the first lines of the five stanzas are enjambed, this method of scanning the first and second lines would seem to be preferred.

Through these slight deviations in the syllabic count and metrical posturing, the poet achieves relief from the rigidity which the flawlessly metrical dimeter line imposes. In fact, Cummings' facility is such that unless we take the time to scan his lines we are not apt to be aware of just how fixed and traditionally established some of his forms are. That he is able to obtain such ease and naturalness of expression within these forms is an indication of his capabilities as a poet in the revered sense of the word. In this particular poem the subtle rhyme scheme that is affixed to the severe metrical pattern bears out this observation.

In each of the stanzas except the third, or middle, stanza there is at least one pair of full end rhymes. In the first stanza the terminal words of the second and fourth line rhyme ("wall" and "all"); in the last stanza which structurally balances with the first we have these same lines (the second and fourth) paired in the same rhyme ("wall" and "fall"). In the second and fourth stanzas, which are again opposites in a pattern of five stanzas, we have the terminal words of the fourth and sixth lines rhyming: in the second stanza "now" and "do"; in the fourth stanza "bough" and "now." These two pairs are partial rhymes. In the third stanza there are two pairs of slant rhymes: "fool" and "steal," "give" and "five." Discounting for the moment the end rhymes of the third and sixth line and the internal rhymes of the last two lines of the final stanza, we have a sound pattern that corresponds with the precision of the metrics in this particular poem. This rhyme pattern can be displayed numerically as follows: 2–4; 4–6; (slant rhymes); 4–6; 2–4.

My sole purpose in belaboring these rather obvious details is to prove Cummings' technical finesse in traditional prosodic forms. The over-all effect of this regularity in rhythm and positioned rhyme makes the poem immediately charming, conveys to the ear of the reader a tone of light-heartedness that corresponds to the natural impulse (unsullied by mental restrictions of any kind) of taking a juicy-looking apple off a tree. But behind this charming, lighthearted tone there is guile, most clearly in evidence, perhaps, in the parenthetical comment that breaks up the easy progression of the poem in a manner that suggests mental caution and reserve and infuses a wary tenseness into the situation being described.

The poem contrasts two perspectives: the naïve versus the sophisticated, the natural instinct to take an apple and eat it versus the legal and moral restrictions placed upon such an act. "Our thief" ("you" or "i" or any innocent child) takes an apple and is caught. He is arraigned ("such fruit" and "what bough"), and he learns that in the perspective of "they" the apples are not simply "red" and "round." He learns that restrictions put upon the apples apply to him. Any similarity between the incident of this poem and the mythical tree of knowledge in Eden is probably intended. Like Adam and Eve the child is forced to submit to an interpretation about apples not inherent in apples. Sin, guilt, punishment are abstractions that are not the properties of apples. Of deities perhaps. Of the mind of man assuredly. But not of apples.

Cummings has said that the tragedy of mankind is the inability of persons to express themselves. In this poem his concept of tragedy is presented in dramatic terms. The stupid perpetuation of injustice may be heard in the repeated vowel sounds and internal rhyme of the last two lines: "with kind of a blind/ big sound on the ground." The apples, regardless of how man perceives them and hence himself, have not altered their basic properties an iota: if they're not eaten, they fall to the ground and rot, completing a natural cycle. The irony in these last two lines asserts that man's tragedy is failure to know truth as it is revealed to him through his senses.

Cummings is a versatile poet, a skilled craftsman. But regardless of what form he employs, from the highly elliptical ideogram to the flawlessly metrical and rhymed stanza, his purpose remains the same: through technique to achieve that precision which conclusively demonstrates the spiritual harmony of the physical universe. At their best, his techniques are the embodiment of his themes.

Epilogue

the harder the wind blows the
taller i am

—no thanks, 55

At the northwest corner of Washington Square stands what Cummings described to me as "newyorkcity's Biggest,so far as am aware,Tree." This fine elm, which he also thought of as a "Beloved Friend," inspired a number of poems. In one of them he ascribed fingers and hands to the tree; "and all the hands," he writes, "have people." This interesting reversal suggests that in an order of importance hands precede people. The metaphor implies the existence of a spiritual harmony that "each particular person" is capable of realizing—but not "people."

Ideally, a man's relation to another man should be like one finger to another on the same hand. A finger is a singularly unique thing: with its fellow fingers it can co-ordinate in harmony. Through his art Cummings dedicated himself to giving dramatic and tangible evidence of the spiritual harmony of the universe made manifest by things visible. A leaf on a tree enjoys an independent existence, yet it is controlled in a larger context by the limbs and boughs of the tree, which determine the place of all the leaves and their relation to each other. Though fixed, each leaf is free in its natural sphere of motion to give expression to its life essence. For Cummings this means birth, growth, fulfillment, and death—a progression in symmetry, harmony, and perfection of love. The presentation of this view of life is the underlying motive behind his poetry and prose.

Ironically, too many people have lost the natural facility to co-ordinate in harmony with each other, as do leaves on a tree or fingers on a hand. Hence the reversal: ideally people should belong to hands. The negation of harmony and vitality results in what Cummings terms an UNworld. In *Adventures in Value,* a book of superb photographs taken by Marion Morehouse, Cummings wrote: "the single business of that UNworld is exploitation:the immediate & ultimate exploitation of everything & everyone,but first & foremost of themselves."

Whether one looks up to Cummings or merely shrugs his shoulders depends, I suppose, upon a willingness to learn to read language and typography as metaphor. My own bias in favor of the precisions and motions of Cummings' poetry is obvious, but how reliable my observations are the reader must decide for himself—perhaps on the basis of the following incident. For some reason I had always thought Cummings was a tall man, taller than I. On leaving his apartment I mentioned my preconception, and we compared our heights. Cummings stood five feet, eight and one half inches tall. I am an inch over six feet.

"Now you can look down on me," he said.

"No. I always thought you were a tall man."

"I'm not, you see. You have probably just been looking up to me."

"Yes," I said, and repeated, rather foolishly, my original conception. I could obviously see that he was not as tall as I had thought him. But prejudices are persistent.

Cummings, who was genial and affable and animated in conversation, joked: "Well, now you can look down on me and all my stuff."

"No, I'd rather look up."

"Yes, that is best," said Cummings.

I am still looking up. He is a tall, tall poet.

Postscript

Since the footnotes in this study are complete with publishing information, a bibliography has not been appended. To date, the following compilations of works by and about Cummings are available to the interested reader: George J. Firmage, ed., *E. E. Cummings: A Miscellany* (New York: Argophile Press, 1958); George J. Firmage, *E. E. Cummings: A Bibliography* (Middletown, Conn.: Wesleyan University Press, 1960); S. V. Baum, ed., ΕΣΤΙ: *e e c, E. E. Cummings and the Critics* (East Lansing: Michigan State University Press, 1961); and Norman Friedman's unpublished but mimeographed *Essays and Reviews Concerning E. E. Cummings*.

A Chronological List of Cummings' Books

The Enormous Room (1922)

Tulips and Chimneys (1923)

& (1925)

XLI Poems (1925)

is 5 (1926)

Him (1927)

[no title] By E. E. Cummings (1930)

CIOPW (1931)

W (ViVa) (1931)

EIMI (1933)

no thanks (1935)

Tom (ballet, 1935)

Collected Poems (1938)

50 Poems (1940)

1 × 1 (1944)

Anthropos: The Future of Art (1944)

Santa Claus: A Morality (1946)

XAIPE (1950)

i:six nonlectures (1953)

Poems: 1923–1954 (1954)

E. E. Cummings: A Miscellany (edited by George Firmage, 1958)

95 Poems (1958)

100 Selected Poems (1959)

Adventures in Value (with Marion Morehouse, 1962)

73 Poems (1963)

E. E. Cummings: A Selection of Poems (with an Introduction by Horace Gregory, 1965)

Index of First Lines of Poems
Referred to in the Text

Subject Index